Economic Freedom of the States of India
2012

Friedrich Naumann STIFTUNG FÜR DIE FREIHEIT

CATO INSTITUTE

INDICUS ANALYTICS

AUTHORS

Bibek Debroy is Professor, Centre for Policy Research, Delhi. He is an economist and has worked in academic institutes and for the government. His primary research interests are education, health, law, governance and trade. He is the author of several books, papers and popular articles.

Laveesh Bhandari, recipient of best thesis award by the EXIM Bank of India in 1996, and Hite Fellowship for work in International Finance. His areas of work are macro-economic research, large-frame surveys on economic and social sectors and consumer profiles, policy analysis, econometric modelling, monitoring and evaluation. His work on inequality, education and India's progress is frequently referred to in the policy debate in India. He has authored and co-authored numerous publications on socioeconomic development, health, education, poverty and inequality.

Swaminathan S. Anklesaria Aiyar is a research fellow at the Cato Institute with a special focus on India and Asia. His research interests include economic change in developing countries, human rights and civil strife, political economy, energy, trade and industry. He is a prolific columnist and TV commentator in India, well-known for a popular weekly column titled "Swaminomics" in the *Times of India*. He is the author of *Escape from the Benevolent Zookeepers: The Best of Swaminomics* (New Delhi: Times of India, 2008) and has been called "India's leading economic journalist" by Stephen Cohen of the Brookings Institution. He has been the editor of India's two biggest financial dailies, *The Economic Times* and *Financial Express*, and was also the India correspondent of *The Economist* for two decades. He has frequently been a consultant to the World Bank and Asian Development Bank. Currently, he is consulting editor of *The Economic Times*. Swami spends part of the year in India and part in the USA. He holds a Master's degree in economics from Oxford University, UK.

Ashok Gulati is Chairman of the Commission for Agricultural Costs and Prices (CACP), Government of India. Before joining CACP, Dr Gulati was Director for more than 10 years in International Food Policy Research Institute (IFPRI). He was also a member of the Economic Advisory Council of the Prime Minister of India.

Economic Freedom of the States of India 2012

Bibek Debroy
Laveesh Bhandari
Swaminathan S. Anklesaria Aiyar
Ashok Gulati

ACADEMIC FOUNDATION
NEW DELHI

First published in 2013 by

Academic Foundation

4772-73 / 23 Bharat Ram Road, (23 Ansari Road), Darya Ganj, New Delhi - 110 002 (India).
Phones : 23245001 / 02 / 03 / 04. Fax : +91-11-23245005. E-mail : books@academicfoundation.com
www : academicfoundation.com

Published in association with :

Friedrich-Naumann-Stiftung für die Freiheit

www.southasia.fnst.org

in partnership with :

Cato Institute

www.cato.org

Indicus Analytics

www.indicus.net

Cataloging in Publication Data--DK
Courtesy: D.K. Agencies (P) Ltd. <docinfo@dkagencies.com>

Economic freedom of the states of India, 2012 / Bibek Debroy ... [et al.].
p. cm.
ISBN 9788171889914
ISBN 8171889913

1. Economic development--India. 2. India--Economic policy--1991- 3. Agriculture and state--India. 4. Manpower policy--India. 5. Free enterprise--India. 6. Economic surveys--India. I. Debroy, Bibek.

DDC 330.954 23

Printed and bound by The Book Mint, New Delhi.
www.thebookmint.in

Contents

Appendices

List of Tables and Figures

TABLES

FIGURES

Foreword

The aim of this report—to measure the level of economic freedom within India—grows out of a larger project begun in the 1980s by the Fraser Institute and culminating in the annual *Economic Freedom of the World* report (co-published by the Cato Institute in the United States). That exercise has proved fruitful in establishing a strong empirical relationship between economic freedom and prosperity, growth, and improvements in the whole range of indicators of human well being. The global report has also produced an explosion of research by leading universities, think tanks and international organisations on the critical role of economic freedom to human progress, including its importance to sustaining civil and political liberty.

The Cato Institute is pleased to co-publish the present report on India with Indicus Analytics and the Friedrich Naumann Foundation at a time when both India's high growth prospects and its commitment to reform have come under scrutiny. The following points come from the data presented here.

- India's economic freedom rating has improved notably since the early 1990s but it is still low and it ranks poorly on a global scale (111th place out of 144 countries).
- The levels of economic freedom from state to state within India vary greatly.
- Numerous states have shown significant increases and significant declines in their economic freedom rankings.
- Greater economic freedom is positively associated with growth at the state level.

Policymakers at the state level can thus draw the strong implication that there is much they can do to improve the welfare of their citizens without having to wait for the central government to implement all policy change. In that regard, one chapter by Swaminathan Aiyar takes an in-depth look at Punjab—a state whose economic freedom rank has fallen notably since 2005—dispels myths about its disappointing performance and points to areas of progress and urgently needed reforms.

Poor policies in two areas—agriculture and the labour sector—could benefit from fundamental reform that would be especially consequential to Indian progress. This year's report includes chapters on each. Ashok Gulati neatly describes the agricultural policy mess that ails India, and he prescribes steps to free farming from its shackles. Bibek Debroy reviews the country's rigid labour regulations and proposes ways states might introduce greater flexibility.

We hope this report can serve policymakers and interested laypersons as a guide to better policies across India.

— Ian Vásquez
Director,
Center for Global Liberty and Prosperity,
Cato Institute

Message

Economic Freedom of the States of India 2012 report demonstrates the significant differences in economic governance that exist in India. It thus has focused attention on state-level reforms to improve inclusive economic growth. The index is based on the Fraser Institute's *Economic Freedom of the World* report. This was developed on the ideas of Milton Friedman, Michael Walker and others who wanted an empirically sound way to measure whether economic freedom would lead to better economic and social outcomes. This has indeed been conclusively demonstrated, and the index has become an important contribution to the international policy debate. Its success has inspired researchers to come up with sub-national indices to capture the performance of subnational institutions in China, Germany and elsewhere. The Friedrich Naumann Stiftung has been engaged in developing an Economic Freedom Index for the States of India for several years now. This index has become an important part of India's reform discourse.

The Indian index is based on the three parameters which are size of the government, legal structure and security of property rights, and regulation of business and labour. The Indian index ranks 20 states of India for which data is available. The researchers have used objective data to produce the Index.

The researchers to the index are distinguished economists from India. Bibek Debroy and Laveesh Bhandari are known for their work in suggesting policy recommendations for Indian economic growth. For the current Index, Cato Institute, a prominent and leading think-tank based in Washington DC has also joined hands. Swaminathan S. Anklesaria Aiyar, a well-known writer and commentator, is the third co-author representing Cato's initiative. This report also has a special chapter authored by

Ashok Gulati on the agricultural reforms in India and the extent of economic freedom in the agricultural sector.

The index shows the direct correlation between economic freedom and the well-being of citizens. As the world index has shown a direct correlation between economic freedom and national indicators of human and material progress, the same similarity is also visible at the subnational level. States in India which are economically more free are also doing better in terms of a higher per capita growth for its citizens, unemployment levels are lower in these states, sanitary conditions are better and the states also attract more investments.

In the current report, we have a special focus on Punjab. Naturally, the state has shown some major fluctuations in its economic growth. The report is a useful instrument for policymakers to observe changes over a time period to understand the benefits and costs of policy changes.

The report is a collaborative effort by the Friedrich Naumann Stifting für die Freiheit, the Cato Institute and the Academic Foundation, New Delhi. We would like to thank all the contributors, authors, partners who have helped in order to make this work see the light of day. We hope it will be a useful tool for research and debate for policymakers and academics alike.

— Siegfried Herzog
Regional Director, South Asia,
Friedrich Naumann Stiftung für die Freiheit

Executive Summary

The *Economic Freedom of the States of India 2012* estimates economic freedom in the 20 biggest Indian states, based on data for 2011, using a methodology adapted from the Fraser Institute's *Economic Freedom of the World* annual reports. The main highlights of this study are as follows.

1. The top state in India in economic freedom in 2011 was Gujarat. It displaced Tamil Nadu, which had been the top state in 2009. Gujarat's freedom index score has been rising fast, and at 0.64 it is now far ahead of second-placed Tamil Nadu (0.56). Madhya Pradesh (0.56) is close behind in third position, Haryana (0.55) retains fourth position and Himachal (0.53) retains fifth position.

2. The bottom three states in 2011 were, in reverse order, Bihar, Jharkhand and West Bengal. In 2009, the reverse order was Bihar, Uttarakhand and Assam. Uttarakhand has moved up sharply from 19th to 14th position, and this improved freedom is reflected in its average GDP growth rate of 12.82 per cent in 2004-2011, the fastest among all states. This is an impressive achievement for a once-backward state.

3. Earlier the median score for economic freedom for all states had declined from 0.38 in 2005 to 0.36 in 2009. But it has now improved substantially to 0.41 in 2011. This is good news. Still the median score lags way behind Gujarat's 0.64, so other states have a long way to go.

4. The biggest improvement has been registered by Madhya Pradesh. Its freedom index score rose from 0.42 in 2009 to 0.56 in 2011, enabling it to move up from 6th to 3rd position. This improved economic freedom was associated with acceleration in its GDP

growth. This averaged 6 per cent per year from 2004-2009, but then accelerated to 9 per cent per year in 2009-2011.

TABLE

Economic Freedom of Indian States: Index Scores and Ranking, 2009 and 2011

	2011 Rank	2009 Rank	2011 Score	2009 Score
Gujarat	1	2	0.64	0.57
Tamil Nadu	2	1	0.57	0.59
Madhya Pradesh	3	6	00.56	0.42
Haryana	4	4	0.55	0.47
Himachal Pradesh	5	5	0.52	0.43
Andhra Pradesh	6	3	0.51	0.51
Jammu and Kashmir	7	8	0.46	0.38
Rajasthan	8	7	0.43	0.40
Karnataka	9	13	0.42	0.34
Kerala	10	10	0.42	0.36
Chhattisgarh	11	15	0.41	0.33
Punjab	12	12	0.39	0.36
Maharashtra	13	10	0.39	0.36
Uttarakhand	14	19	0.38	0.26
Assam	15	18	0.36	0.29
Uttar Pradesh	16	13	0.35	0.34
Orissa	17	17	0.34	0.31
West Bengal	18	15	0.32	0.33
Jharkhand	19	8	0.31	0.38
Bihar	20	20	0.29	0.23

5. The biggest decline in economic freedom has been recorded by Jharkhand, which slumped from 8th to 19th position. Its score declined from 0.38 to 0.31. Unsurprisingly, its GDP growth has averaged only 4.6 per cent in 2004-2011, one of the lowest among all states (see Table 1.8). Jharkhand has special problems as a heavily forested state suffering from Maoist insurrections. But such problems also afflict its southern neighbour, Chhattisgarh, which has jumped up from 15th to 11th position in economic freedom. The state has been rewarded with rapid GDP growth averaging 10.0 per cent per year in 2004-2011.

6. As many as eight states have registered a decline in rank. These include some of the most industrialised states, such as Tamil Nadu, Maharashtra and Andhra Pradesh. However, the situation is better than it sounds. Some of these states have improved their freedom scores (Maharashtra, Rajasthan), but nevertheless fallen in rankings, because other states have improved their scores even faster.

7. Seen over a longer time horizon, Punjab has fallen in economic freedom rankings from 6th position in 2005 to 12th position in 2011. Once among the most prosperous and fast-growing states, it has suffered relative decline. This cannot be explained either by Sikh militancy (which ended two decades ago) or tensions with Pakistan, two favourite explanations trotted out by the state's politicians. Punjab's travails arise mainly from high fiscal deficits and public debt, both arising substantially from the curse of free rural electricity given to woo farmers' votes. Perverse incentives and money laundering have driven land prices so high as to inhibit industrial investment. However, the recent opening up of trade with Pakistan promises to convert Punjab into India's gateway to Pakistan, and this could help accelerate the state's growth. Punjab's investment climate has positive features: Ludhiana is ranked the best city in India in ease of doing business by the *Doing Business* series of the IFC/World Bank. The state's shift from government monopolies to public-private partnerships (PPPs) has facilitated increased investment in power, roads, education and health.

8. This report includes a special chapter on economic freedom in agriculture. Indian agriculture is bound hand and foot, and cries out for freedom. Not only is the production and marketing of sugar subject to extensive central and state controls, even the production and pricing of by-products (molasses, electricity, ethanol, chemicals) are subject to multiple controls. Even packaging (in jute bags, not plastic bags) is controlled. Other crops suffering from a plethora of prohibitions and controls are rice, fruit and vegetables. Land and water, the primary inputs for agriculture, are also subject to many restrictions and controls. This lack of freedom hurts farmers and keeps them disempowered and poor.

9. A special chapter on the labour market highlights the lack of reform in labour laws, and their adverse impact on economic freedom and growth. Among the states, Maharashtra has the best labour regulation, followed by Karnataka and Punjab. The worst states are West Bengal, Kerala, Uttar Pradesh and Assam. Job growth is concentrated in self-employment, a lot in informal sectors like street hawking, since labour laws discourage hiring by corporations, and encourage capital intensity and minimisation of labour use. Rigid labour laws explain why India has failed to set up huge factories for labour-intensive exports, something that many Asian countries used as a launching pad for economic growth. India also needs to eliminate obsolete labour laws (such as those mandating manual

rather than electronic registers), and laws limiting hours of work for shops or female employment. If labour issues are shifted from the concurrent list to the states list, then those states wishing to reform can go ahead without waiting for central legislation, which is difficult in these times of political gridlock.

1

The State of Economic Freedom in India

Bibek Debroy and Laveesh Bhandari

This report is the latest in our series of reports measuring economic freedom in different states of India. *Economic Freedom of the States of India* (EFSI), 2012, uses data relating mainly to 2011. Economic freedom isn't the only kind of freedom: political liberties and civil rights are also notions of freedom. Freedom House ranks countries in the world on the basis of such liberties and rights.[1] However, we seek to measure economic freedom alone, drawing on the methodology already established in *Economic Freedom of the World* (EFW), an annual publication of The Fraser Institute (co-published in the United States by the Cato Institute), that has been brought out since 1996. Some of the parameters measured in EFW, such as sound money or international trade, have meaning only at the national level: all state governments are bound by New Delhi's monetary and international trade policies. So, while taking a lead from the methodology of EFW, we have adapted it in our own report, EFSI 2012. The full details of the methodology are given in the appendix.

Table 1.1 shows how India scores in the 2012 EFW ratings, with data up to 2010. This shows that economic freedom rose from a index score of just 5.15 in 1980 to a peak of 6.72 in 2005, but has since declined a bit to 6.26 in 2010. Only in respect of international trade has freedom increased continuously. It has decreased between 2005 and 2010 for the other four parameters of EFW: size of government, legal system and property rights, sound money, and regulation. India ranks only 111st out of 144 countries in the EFW list, having slipped from 76th position in 2005. Clearly its government has attached a low priority to improving economic freedom.

TABLE 1.1

India's Scores in Economic Freedom of the World

	1980	1985	1990	1995	2000	2005	2009	2010
Summary rating	5.15	4.83	4.89	5.76	6.32	6.72	6.31	6.26
Size of government	5.00	4.50	4.88	6.26	6.83	7.42	6.33	6.37
Legal structure & security of property rights	5.78	4.92	4.39	5.87	5.99	6.51	5.78	5.55
Access to sound money	6.29	6.61	6.63	6.50	6.88	6.84	6.55	6.42
Freedom to trade internationally	3.00	2.40	2.67	4.50	5.51	6.07	6.20	6.28
Regulation of credit, labour & business	5.68	5.70	5.87	5.66	6.40	6.74	6.68	6.70

Source: Economic Freedom of the World 2012 (unadjusted series, p.88).

The good news is that economic freedom in the states of India has improved even though it has slipped at the national level. In other words, state capitals have been doing more to improve economic freedom than New Delhi. The median value of our economic freedom index is up from 0.38 in 2005 to 0.41 in 2011. Gujarat has shown a remarkable increase from 0.46 to 0.64, and has moved up from 5th position in 2005 to become India's top state in economic freedom today. However some other states have slipped back, the worst performer being Jharkhand, from 0.40 to 0.31 (see Table 1.2). Bihar has improved significantly from 0.25 to 0.29, but remains last in the table.

TABLE 1.2

Overall Economic Freedom Ratings 2011

	2005		2009		2011	
States	*Overall*	*Rank*	*Overall*	*Rank*	*Overall*	*Rank*
Gujarat	0.46	5	0.57	2	0.64	1
Tamil Nadu	0.57	1	0.59	1	0.57	2
Madhya Pradesh	0.49	2	0.42	6	0.56	3
Haryana	0.47	4	0.47	4	0.55	4
Himachal Pradesh	0.48	3	0.43	5	0.52	5
Andhra Pradesh	0.40	7	0.51	3	0.51	6
Jammu & Kashmir	0.34	15	0.38	8	0.46	7
Rajasthan	0.37	12	0.40	7	0.43	8
Karnataka	0.36	13	0.34	13	0.42	9
Kerala	0.38	10	0.36	10	0.42	10
Chhattisgarh	0.33	16	0.33	15	0.41	11
Punjab	0.41	6	0.35	12	0.39	12
Maharashtra	0.40	9	0.36	10	0.39	13
Uttaranchal	0.33	17	0.26	19	0.38	14
Assam	0.30	19	0.29	18	0.36	15
Uttar Pradesh	0.35	14	0.34	13	0.35	16
Orissa	0.37	11	0.31	17	0.34	17
West Bengal	0.31	18	0.33	15	0.32	18
Jharkhand	0.40	8	0.38	8	0.31	19
Bihar	0.25	20	0.23	20	0.29	20

Our economic freedom index is constructed drawing on EFW's methodology, and thus ensures that the economic freedom rating for Indian states has measures that are somewhat comparable with those of other countries. However, given Indian conditions and the sharing of responsibilities between the states and the central government, only three of the five areas are found to be appropriate where the state governments have powers to directly impact conditions and institutions (see Table 1.3). These are:

- Size of government: expenditures, taxes and enterprises.
- Legal structure and security of property rights.
- Regulation of labour and business.

TABLE 1.3

Areas under Central and State Government Control

Under State Control	*Under Central Control*	*Under Common Control*
Law, order, justice and local governance	Administrative functions such as defence, foreign affairs	Interstate interactions
Public health and environment	Labour, quality standards	Labour issues
Land and water	Railways, shipping, ports, airports, post & telegraph	Education
Some types of taxes	Income tax, customs and excise	Environment
Infrastructure except national highways	Deals with the RBI, pubic debt	Power
Some aspects related to commerce & industry	Natural resources	Shipping and inland waterways

The index of economic freedom however is calculated for each of these categories, and then aggregated. Each category is important for indicating a specific aspect of economic freedom.

While the categories have been included in the index on the lines of the *Economic Freedom of the World* reports, the variables from the EFW could not be replicated at the subnational level in India. So proxies have been taken wherever possible that are more meaningful at the state level. Often data were unavailable, in which case those indicators had to be eliminated from the study. A detailed table that correlates the indicators used in EFW and those included in the study is presented in the appendix. We give below the methodology in brief: a fuller, more detailed account can be found in the appendix.

Methodology in Brief

Since data needs to be comparable across time and geography, credible and robust, and highly reflective of the conditions in different states the following criteria have been identified in the selection of variables.

1. The data should be objective: that is, it should not be based on perceptions but on hard facts such that it is not sensitive to perceptions of elite groups or the masses but should reflect conditions as they actually are

2. The data should be available from highly respected, public and ideally government or semi-government sources: this would ensure that the ensuing discussion and debate should focus on the resultant performance of the states and not on the quality and credibility of the data

3. The data should be available periodically and should be available from the same source for different states: this would ensure the credibility of the data and the continuity of the ratings

Each of the variables that are constructed is normalised to correct for the differences in the size of the states. Hence normalisation is done by dividing by population, area, a ratio or using it as a percentage of some aggregate so that it is neutral to the size of the state. Moreover, each data source needs to be available for a large enough number of states so that missing data points are minimised.

In line with the previous ratings for the Indian states, the range equalisation with equal weights has been chosen as the appropriate method. This is a multi-stage process. First, range equalisation is conducted on each variable across all states—this requires the subtraction of the minimum value from the value for each state and dividing the resultant with the difference of the maximum and minimum values. Range equalisation ensures that all variables lie between 0 and 1. Each of the new 'range equalised' variables is then aggregated with others using equal weights to create an index for each of the areas under consideration. Next the indices of each of the three areas are aggregated to obtain a composite index using equal weights. Thus, four indices are generated on which basis each of the states is ranked.

Area 1: Size of Government: Expenditures, Taxes and Enterprises

Interference of the government in the functioning of the economy or a large role of the government as a producer and provider of services and goods or of redistribution of resources reduces the level of economic freedom. Government revenue expenditure, administrative GDP and a large employment in the public sector are therefore indicators of size of the government. Taxes on income, commodities and services, property and capital transactions, and other duties are indicative of the extensive role played by the government in the economy.

1) Inverse of government revenue expenditure as a share of gross state domestic product (GSDP)

Higher revenue expenditure by the government is indicative of a large size of the government and thus an indicator of lower economic freedom. Therefore, inverse of this ratio has been considered.

2) Inverse of administrative GSDP as a ratio of total GSDP

Administrative GDP is the contribution of government services to the national product. The lower this ratio, the better is the level of economic freedom as the government's role is lower; therefore the inverse of this ratio is used.

3) Inverse of share of government in organised employment

This is the ratio of employment with the government and quasi-government institutions to total organised sector employment. This ratio is a direct indicator of the size of the government. Inverse of the ratio is considered.

4) Inverse of state level taxes on income as a ratio of GDP

This is the ratio of income tax collected by the state to the GDP. The lower the state taxes on income, higher will be the economic freedom. So, the inverse of this ratio has been incorporated in the analysis.

5) Inverse of ratio of state level taxes on property and capital transactions to state GDP

This is the ratio of taxes on property and capital transactions to state GDP. High transaction costs and taxes tend to restrict the trade activities. Therefore, economic freedom is considered to be inversely related to level of taxation and the inverse of the variable has been taken.

6) Inverse of state level taxes on commodities and services to GDP

This is the ratio of taxes collected on commodities and services i.e., sales tax, service tax, excise, etc. to the GDP. Lower taxes on commodities would result in a higher freedom index; therefore the inverse of this ratio has been used.

7) Inverse of Stamp duty rate

Stamp duty is defined as tax collected by the state by requiring a stamp to be purchased and attached on the commodity. Higher duties impose higher constraints on trade and economic activities and curb the economic freedom of agents. The inverse of this variable is taken to ensure that higher level of economic freedom is reflected by a higher ratio.

TABLE 1.4

Size of Government: State Ratings and Rankings

	2005		2009		2011	
States	*Area 1*	*Rank*	*Area 1*	*Rank*	*Area 1*	*Rank*
Haryana	0.50	7	0.63	3	0.75	1
Gujarat	0.56	2	0.69	1	0.74	2
Maharashtra	0.52	5	0.53	6	0.68	3
Assam	0.41	11	0.51	7	0.63	4
Jammu & Kashmir	0.31	20	0.43	14	0.63	5
Punjab	0.49	8	0.54	5	0.61	6
West Bengal	0.52	4	0.58	4	0.61	7
Andhra Pradesh	0.39	12	0.49	8	0.58	8
Tamil Nadu	0.46	9	0.47	11	0.57	9
Himachal Pradesh	0.58	1	0.48	10	0.56	10
Bihar	0.38	16	0.44	12	0.54	11
Kerala	0.51	6	0.49	8	0.54	12
Chhattisgarh	0.37	17	0.32	19	0.53	13
Jharkhand	0.56	3	0.67	2	0.50	14
Rajasthan	0.34	18	0.44	12	0.50	15
Karnataka	0.38	15	0.36	16	0.48	16
Uttaranchal	0.39	13	0.25	20	0.45	17
Orissa	0.32	19	0.38	15	0.44	18
Madhya Pradesh	0.39	14	0.35	17	0.42	19
Uttar Pradesh	0.45	10	0.33	18	0.40	20

Haryana has been the most rapidly growing state of India and has also attracted large investments. The state is attracting significant investments in the services sector and in manufacturing. Proximity to Delhi, one of India's fastest growing economic centres would have helped, but Haryana has been able to leverage it without too much increase in government (see Table 1.4).

Gujarat's is a well-known success story through much of the 2000s. Moreover it has had major successes in agriculture, social welfare programmes, water resource management. All of this is being achieved without an inordinate increase in the size of the government.

Maharashtra is another state that is among the better performers in this area; the size of the government has not increased as much as economic growth in recent years. Assam's index values and rankings show that there has been significant improvement but here as well, the data shows many year-on-year variations—largely due to an economy that is highly dependent upon agriculture. Jammu & Kashmir is now among the best performers in this area with a low size of government and relatively high economic growth. But it should be noted that the policing functions and manpower are not adequately captured in state-level data since there is a large element of central force deployment in the state. The index values of 2005 and 2009 show that the state was amongst the poorest performers.

But Jharkhand is another story. The declining index values and relative ranking of Jharkhand in this area only confirm the much stated worsening condition in recent years. Its human development indicators are among the poorest in the country (*India Today,* "State of the States Rankings", various years). And it is currently at the centre of a large leftist violent movement. Uttar Pradesh is the worst performer in this area owing to a larger increase in taxation in comparison with slower economic growth.

Tamil Nadu and Bihar have shown steady improvement in their index values and relative ranking—each has benefitted from economic growth without commensurate increase in the size of their government.

Overall there has been some improvement in this category in the period 2005 to 2011, with the average values increasing from 0.39 in 2005 to 0.47 in 2009 and to 0.56 in 2011.

Area 2: Legal Structure and Security of Property Rights

The efficiency of the government in protecting human life and property is measured by this category. The quality of the justice mechanism is measured by the availability of judges, by the completion rate of cases by courts and investigations by the police. The level of safety in the region is measured by the recovery rate of stolen property and by the rate of violent and economic crimes.

8) *Ratio of total value of property recovered to total value of property stolen*

One of the key ingredients of economic freedom is protection of property. This is the ratio of total value of property recovered to the total value of property stolen. A higher value of this variable denotes efficiency of law enforcing agencies in protecting property rights and would therefore signify greater economic freedom.

9) Inverse of violent crimes as a share of total crimes

This is the ratio of violent crimes, including murder, attempt to murder, etc., to total crimes under the Indian Penal Code (IPC). The inverse of this ratio is considered, relating higher economic freedom to lower incidence of violent crimes.

10) Inverse of cases under economic offences as a share of total cases registered

This is the ratio of economic offences (criminal breach of trust and cheating) to the total crimes reported under the IPC. Inverse of this ratio is considered, as lower incidence of economic offences is indicative of better protection of property rights and therefore higher economic freedom.

11) Inverse of vacant posts of judges in the judiciary as a ratio of total sanctioned posts of judges

This is the ratio of total vacant posts of judges in district/subordinate courts to total posts sanctioned. A high value of the ratio indicates that adequate infrastructure for getting justice is not in place. Therefore, the inverse of this ratio is considered.

12) Percentage cases where investigations were completed by police

This is the ratio of total cases where investigations were completed by the police to total cases registered for investigation by them. A higher value of this ratio indicates higher economic freedom as it indicates lower pendency of investigations.

13) Percentage cases where trials were completed by courts

This is the ratio of total trials completed by the courts to total cases awaiting or undergoing trial by courts. A higher value indicates higher economic freedom as it indicates lower pendency of cases.

Madhya Pradesh is one of the best governed states and this is reflected in its index value that is far ahead of all others (see Table 1.5). Better police investigations as well as a lower share of economic offences to the total incidences of crime resulted in significant improvement over time in the state. On the other hand, significant decline is noticed in the index values of Tamil Nadu. The state is at a distant second.

TABLE 1.5

Legal Structure and Security: State Ratings and Rankings

	2005		2009		2011	
States	*Area 2*	*Rank*	*Area 2*	*Rank*	*Area 2*	*Rank*
Madhya Pradesh	0.63	2	0.62	2	0.83	1
Tamil Nadu	0.80	1	0.90	1	0.64	2
Rajasthan	0.49	5	0.54	4	0.53	3
Gujarat	0.35	12	0.54	4	0.52	4
Andhra Pradesh	0.48	7	0.56	3	0.49	5
Kerala	0.35	13	0.34	10	0.45	6
Chhattisgarh	0.48	6	0.52	6	0.43	7
Haryana	0.58	3	0.45	7	0.42	8
Himachal Pradesh	0.51	4	0.42	8	0.41	9
Uttar Pradesh	0.41	10	0.39	9	0.38	10
Punjab	0.42	9	0.34	10	0.38	11
Karnataka	0.45	8	0.34	10	0.36	12
Uttaranchal	0.28	15	0.29	14	0.31	13
Jammu & Kashmir	0.35	14	0.32	13	0.29	14
Orissa	0.37	11	0.23	16	0.26	15
Jharkhand	0.19	18	0.24	15	0.17	16
Assam	0.14	19	0.17	18	0.17	17
West Bengal	0.2	17	0.15	19	0.16	18
Maharashtra	0.26	16	0.19	17	0.15	19
Bihar	0.12	20	0.11	20	0.08	20

Rajasthan's ratings show an improvement since 2005. The value of property recovered out of property stolen and decline in the proportion of violent crime are some of the factors leading to its improvement. However, in the period 2009 to 2011, there has been a marginal decline in the state's rating. Kerala's improvement has been quite marked largely because of improvement in terms of reduced vacancy of judges. Also, there has been a significant decline in the cases under economic offence.

However many states have shown a fall in overall ratings in this area since 2009—Tamil Nadu, Chhattisgarh, Andhra Pradesh, Jharkhand, Maharashtra and Haryana, all show significant declines in index values. This is worrisome as some of these states like Jharkhand and Maharashtra were among the poor performers in 2009 as well.

The ratings reflect that as Gujarat leaves behind its sordid past of communal violence and destruction, other states are unable to improve security of life and property in the manner required. This puts a serious question mark on the sustainability of high economic growth in such states.

Area 3: Regulation of Labour and Business

An entrepreneur needs to take many decisions that cannot cater to the sentiments of all the workers and management that his firm employs. Decisions such as rationalisation of employee strength are an essential component of efficient use of scarce resources. Constraints on exiting seriously hamper an entrepreneur's freedom. Labour laws for many decades have favoured the rights of the workers in the country. The number of strikes and industrial disputes that take place in the economy portray the amount of economic freedom in terms of the control that an entrepreneur has over his own business. Other areas where an entrepreneur may lack control over his own business is in terms of lack of adequate infrastructure and raw material. Such limitations severely constrain the entrepreneur's ability to enforce decisions that may be beneficial for his business. High transaction costs are well known deterrents of trade and economic activity. They also contribute to black market transactions. The higher the costs in terms of licenses, the more constraints they impose on carrying out trade and economic activity and therefore serve as restraints on economic freedom of agents. Corruption also translates into higher transactions costs.

14) Ratio of average wage of unskilled workers (males) to minimum wages

This is the ratio of yearly average of daily wages for harvesting to minimum agricultural wages in the state. A higher than one ratio in a state indicates that the wages received by workers are higher than the specified minimum implying greater economic freedom both for the entrepreneur and labour.

15) Ratio of average wage of unskilled workers (females) to minimum wages

This is the ratio of yearly average of daily female wages for harvesting to minimum agricultural wages in the state. A higher than one ratio in a state indicates that the wages received by workers is higher than the specified minimum implying greater economic freedom both for the entrepreneur and labour. This ratio is taken separately from that for males as many times the market determined wages for unskilled female workers are said to be biased against them.

16) Inverse of man-days lost in strikes and lockouts/total number of industrial workers

This is the ratio of man-days lost due to disputes (strikes and lockouts) to the total number of workers. A large number of man-days lost indicates the breakdown in arbitration and other consensus mechanisms. The fewer the man-days lost, the better is economic freedom. Therefore, the inverse of this variable is considered.

17) Implementation rate of industrial entrepreneurs memorandum (IEM)

IEM denotes the intention to invest in an industry. However, when there are bureaucratic or other delays, the rate of implementation is low. This indicator is the ratio of total amount invested to total amount proposed for investment in the shape of IEMs. A higher ratio implies larger economic freedom and thus depicting lower interference of government.

18) Inverse of minimum license fee for traders

Traders are required to pay a minimum amount of fees for obtaining a license from the government to indulge in market activities. Therefore, the higher the license fees, the more restricted traders are while trading in the market. The inverse of the variable is taken to denote higher levels of economic freedom.

19) Inverse of power shortage as a percentage of total demand

This is the ratio of power shortage to the total demand for power. Power shortage exists either due to low investment on the part of the government or due to low levels of private sector generation. A higher power shortage will tend to slow down the production process and thus would relate directly to inability of an entrepreneur to control his business. Again, the inverse of the ratio is taken.

20) Inverse of pendency rate of cases registered under corruption and related acts

This is the ratio of cases pending investigation from the previous year of cases registered under the Prevention of Corruption Act and other related acts as a share of total cases registered under the same acts. Economic freedom is higher when justice is served promptly and therefore the inverse of the pendency rate is used.

Gujarat has seen significant improvement in its index values and retains its pre-eminent position (see Table 1.6). Himachal Pradesh has seen the most significant improvement in this measure. This position of Himachal Pradesh is contributed by better performance on a range of variables—yearly market wages to minimum notified wages for unskilled workers, strikes and lock outs, and total cases registered in the prevention of corruption act improved.

TABLE 1.6

Regulation of Labour and Business: State Ratings and Rankings

	2005		2009		2011	
States	*Area 5*	*Rank*	*Area 5*	*Rank*	*Area 5*	*Rank*
Gujarat	0.47	1	0.49	1	0.67	1
Himachal Pradesh	0.36	7	0.38	5	0.63	2
Tamil Nadu	0.46	2	0.41	3	0.51	3
Jammu & Kashmir	0.35	8	0.39	4	0.48	4
Haryana	0.32	11	0.34	7	0.47	5
Andhra Pradesh	0.33	10	0.48	2	0.45	6
Madhya Pradesh	0.46	3	0.27	11	0.44	7
Karnataka	0.24	17	0.32	8	0.43	8
Uttaranchal	0.31	12	0.24	14	0.40	9
Maharashtra	0.41	6	0.35	6	0.36	10
Orissa	0.43	5	0.31	9	0.33	11
Assam	0.34	9	0.19	17	0.28	12
Uttar Pradesh	0.18	19	0.3	10	0.28	13
Chhattisgarh	0.14	20	0.14	20	0.28	14
Kerala	0.28	15	0.25	12	0.27	15
Rajasthan	0.28	14	0.22	16	0.25	16
Bihar	0.26	16	0.15	19	0.24	17
Jharkhand	0.45	4	0.24	14	0.24	18
West Bengal	0.2	18	0.25	12	0.24	19
Punjab	0.3	13	0.18	18	0.22	20

Madhya Pradesh, Tamil Nadu and Uttaranchal had a major decline in the period 2005 to 2009. In each of these states significant recovery is noticed in 2011. This has been on the back of better performance in a range of variables—yearly wage to minimum notified wages, actual investment to investment proposed and total cases registered in the Prevention of Corruption Act, have all improved. Assam has also improved in this measure. The state's performance on ratio of industrial workers to strikes and lock outs has enabled it to substantially improve upon its low ranking in 2009.

Uttar Pradesh had a low ranking in 2005 (at 19) and has improved upon it in 2009. One of the factors behind this is better performance in the variable registration of cases under Prevention of Corruption Act. However, in 2011 there had been a reversal in the performance of the state.

Jharkhand has performed poorly in 2011 and has declined in its rank, but its poor performance has been in a range of areas—yearly wages to minimum notified wages, total industrial workers to strikes and lock outs, total cases registered in the Prevention of Corruption Act, all have declined. West Bengal and Punjab are the other two states that have shown significant declines in their ranks since 2009. A range of factors account for the decline in their performance, the most important of which is the decline in the proportion of cases registered under the Prevention of Corruption Act.

In the regulation of labour and business category, the average state value had decreased in the first two time points i.e., 0.39 in 2005 to 0.30 in 2009. In 2011, the average state value increased to 0.35. With an exception of Andhra Pradesh, Uttar Pradesh and West Bengal, all the other states have improved in this measure since 2009.

Overall Ratings

The overall ratings are a simple equal weighted average of the three ratings and the top three states are Gujarat, Tamil Nadu and Madhya Pradesh (see Table 1.7). These are followed by Haryana and Himachal Pradesh. Gujarat has significantly improved in its rating from 0.47 in 2005 to 0.64 in 2011, mainly driven by better legal and regulatory performance. Tamil Nadu has been a consistent performer—it was at the top in 2005 as well as 2009 but has declined to second rank in 2011. In the case of Madhya Pradesh as well the improvement from 0.42 in 2009 to 0.56 has enabled it to achieve a rank of 3. The improvement in Madhya Pradesh largely stems from the legal structure. Among the top 5, while Haryana retains its 4th position Andhra Pradesh has slipped from 3rd to 6th position in rankings.

As many as eight states have seen a fall in their economic freedom rankings since 2005. The worst performers in 2011 are Jharkhand, West Bengal and Maharashtra. Jharkhand is one state that has performed poorly, its rating has fallen by 0.09 since 2005. The other states with declining index values since 2005 are Orissa, Maharashtra and Punjab. On the other end, Bihar has not been able to break out of the bottom position it has held for so many years, despite an improvement in its ratings. If the same improvement momentum continues it is expected to finally break out of its laggard position the time the next ratings are conducted.

Overall, the median value for economic freedom of the states of India decreased from 0.38 in 2005 to 0.36 in 2009 but improved thereafter to 0.41 in 2011. The increase in the overall index values is the consequence of improvement in all the three measures, i.e., size of the government, legal structure and property rights, and regulation of labour and business. In other words, the evidence is that economic freedom in India has improved since 2009.

TABLE 1.7

Overall Economic Freedom Ratings, 2011

	2005		2009		2011	
States	*Overall*	*Rank*	*Overall*	*Rank*	*Overall*	*Rank*
Gujarat	0.46	5	0.57	2	0.64	1
Tamil Nadu	0.57	1	0.59	1	0.57	2
Madhya Pradesh	0.49	2	0.42	6	0.56	3
Haryana	0.47	4	0.47	4	0.55	4
Himachal Pradesh	0.48	3	0.43	5	0.52	5
Andhra Pradesh	0.4	7	0.51	3	0.51	6
Jammu & Kashmir	0.34	15	0.38	8	0.46	7
Rajasthan	0.37	12	0.4	7	0.43	8
Karnataka	0.36	13	0.34	13	0.42	9
Kerala	0.38	10	0.36	10	0.42	10
Chhattisgarh	0.33	16	0.33	15	0.41	11
Punjab	0.41	6	0.35	12	0.39	12
Maharashtra	0.4	9	0.36	10	0.39	13
Uttarakhand	0.33	17	0.26	19	0.38	14
Assam	0.3	19	0.29	18	0.36	15
Uttar Pradesh	0.35	14	0.34	13	0.35	16
Orissa	0.37	11	0.31	17	0.34	17
West Bengal	0.31	18	0.33	15	0.32	18
Jharkhand	0.4	8	0.38	8	0.31	19
Bihar	0.25	20	0.23	20	0.29	20

As India opens its national markets to international investment and commodity flows, it cannot afford to constrain its own entrepreneurs from benefitting from the great opportunities that lie ahead. For this, economic freedom needs to be improved at the national, state and local levels.

A Discussion of Economic Freedom in the States of India

Overall the states of Jharkhand and Orissa have had a significant fall in their economic freedom ratings. Others such as Punjab, Maharashtra and Tamil Nadu have had a moderate fall in their ratings (reduction of between 0 to 0.02 points). While Gujarat, Jammu & Kashmir and Andhra Pradesh have seen a significant improvement (improvement from 0.11 to 0.18 points); Chhattisgarh, Haryana, Madhya Pradesh, Karnataka, Assam, Rajasthan, Uttarakhand, Himachal Pradesh, Bihar, Kerala, West Bengal and Uttar Pradesh have seen a moderate improvement (0 to 0.08 points).

But the states that have improved the most have seen improvements on a whole range of indicators. This suggests that improvements in economic freedom can be most dramatic when they are comprehensive and not driven by excellent performance in just one or two areas.

There is a link between economic freedom and economic growth, although the correlations are not as high as in our reports for previous years. The states that have worsened most saw an average annual GDP growth between 2004-05 and 2009-10 of 7 per cent. At the same time, the states that improved the most grew at 9.3 per cent on the average.

Table 1.8 shows the link between growth and freedom; apart from the moderate fall states (all of which showed a high ranking in the past) improved economic freedom is linked with higher growth rates in the

TABLE 1.8

Economic Growth and Economic Freedom in Indian States

States	*GSDP at 2004-05 Price (Rs. '000 crore) in 2004-05*	*GSDP at 2004-05 Price (Rs. '000 crore) in 2010-11*	*Annual % Growth*	*Index Values of 2005*	*Rank in 2005*	*Index Values in 2011*	*Rank in 2011*	*Change in EFI (2005 to 2011)*	*Change in Rank (2005 to 2011)*	*Position in 2005*
Jharkhand	60	78	4.60	0.40	8	0.31	19	-0.09	-11	High
Orissa	77	127	8.80	0.37	11	0.34	17	-0.03	-6	Low
States with Large Decline	**136**	**205**	**7.00**							
Punjab	97	150	7.60	0.41	6	0.40	12	-0.02	-6	High
Maharashtra	414	775	11.00	0.40	9	0.40	13	-0.01	-4	High
Tamil Nadu	219	391	10.20	0.57	1	0.57	2	0.00	-1	High
States with Moderate Decline	**633**	**1,166**	**10.70**							
Uttar Pradesh	261	397	7.30	0.35	14	0.36	16	0	-2	Low
West Bengal	209	314	7.00	0.31	18	0.33	18	0.01	0	Low
Kerala	119	197	8.70	0.38	10	0.42	10	0.04	-1	Low
Bihar	78	142	10.60	0.25	20	0.29	20	0.04	0	Low
Himachal Pradesh	24	39	8.40	0.48	3	0.53	5	0.04	-2	High
Uttaranchal	25	52	13.20	0.33	17	0.38	14	0.05	3	Low
Rajasthan	128	196	7.40	0.37	12	0.43	8	0.06	3	Low
Assam	53	75	5.80	0.30	19	0.36	15	0.06	4	Low
Karnataka	166	271	8.50	0.36	13	0.43	9	0.06	3	Low
Madhya Pradesh	113	170	7.10	0.49	2	0.56	3	0.07	-1	High
Haryana	95	165	9.60	0.47	4	0.55	4	0.08	0	High
Chhattisgarh	48	85	10.00	0.33	16	0.41	11	0.08	4	Low
States with Moderate Rise	**474**	**776**	**8.60**							
Andhra Pradesh	225	372	8.80	0.40	7	0.51	6	0.11	1	High
Jammu & Kashmir	27	38	5.80	0.34	15	0.46	7	0.12	8	Low
Gujarat	203	364	10.20	0.46	5	0.64	1	0.18	4	High
States with Large Rise	**455**	**775**	**9.30**					-		

aggregate. The outlier, the moderate fall states, also indicates that higher economic freedom generates a momentum growth that has a long term positive impact. It also suggests that our freedom indicators are unable to capture some of the gains made in states like Bihar, where Chief Minister Nitish Kumar dramatically improved the business climate through mass arrests of mafia gangsters.

End Note

1. *http://www.freedomhouse.org.*

2

Why Punjab has Suffered Long, Steady Decline

Swaminathan S. Anklesaria Aiyar

Introduction

Punjab has historically been one of the fastest-growing and richest states of India, with one of the lowest poverty rates. Punjab's farmers are the best in India, boasting the highest rice and wheat yields. The state was at the very heart of the green revolution which, starting in the mid-1960s, ended Indian starvation and heavy dependence on food aid. Punjab was among the first states to provide weather-proof roads and electricity to all villages, these being important facilitators of the green revolution. Electricity was required to provide irrigation through tubewells, and good roads were essential to move inputs to farms and produce out to markets. Punjab has always boasted a tradition of entrepreneurship and willingness to travel to other states and countries in search of work. This has produced a large return stream of cash remittances, estimated to be the second largest of any state after Kerala.[1]

However, since the 1980s the state has lost its economic leadership among states and steadily slipped behind other states. In the budget speech introducing the state budget for 2011-12, the Punjab Finance Minister said, "I must mention that on the basis of per capita income, Punjab which was at one time the top State in the country has slipped to number four among the bigger states and to number eight if all the states and union territories are reckoned. Punjab cannot be satisfied with anything but the first place in this regard."[2]

Since the 1990s (see Table 2.1), Punjab's GDP growth has been lower than the national average. According to government data (CSO estimate, November 2011), the state's GDP growth in 1994-2002 was 4.32 per cent per year, against the national average of 6.16 per cent; and in the period 2002-2011, Punjab's rate was 6.61 per cent against the national 7.95 per cent. By global standards, these were reasonable rates of growth. But relative to other Indian states, Punjab kept slipping.[3]

TABLE 2.1

Growth of State GDP

(Per cent)

	1994-95 to 2001-02	*2002-03 to 2010-11*
Punjab	4.32	6.61
Rajasthan	7.36	6.83
Gujarat	6.45	10.42
Haryana	6.47	9.17
Chhattisgarh	3.16	9.19
Himachal Pradesh	6.81	7.91
Uttrakhand	4.61	12.21
All India	6.16	7.95

Source: Central Statistical Organisation Databook, November 1st, 2011.

A major weakness has been a high fiscal deficit, which is the highest among all major states—budgeted at 3.4 per cent of GDP for 2011-12. The high fiscal deficit arises mainly out of huge unwarranted subsidies, the chief culprit being free power to farmers. One consequence is that the government is not even able to pay all salaries on time. This leads to demoralisation and cynicism among staff, who look for avenues to make money illegally.[4]

As measured by the Economic Freedom Index (EFI) in this report, Punjab's rank has slipped badly from 6th position in 2005 to 12th position in 2011. This does not reflect a major deterioration in its freedom rating, which has dipped just marginally from 0.41 to 0.39. But it has failed to keep up with other states, many of whom have improved their freedom ratings dramatically. Gujarat, the freest state, has gone up from 0.46 to 0.64. Haryana, which used to be the most backward part of Punjab until it split away in the 1960s, has improved its index value from 0.47 to 0.55, and has consistently ranked as the fourth-freest state from 2005 to 2011. This drives home the overall story of Punjab's steady relative decline, even though in absolute terms its performance has not been too bad.

However, there is one clear silver lining. At the local level, Punjab's cities have created a relatively good business climate. Ludhiana, the biggest city in the state, is reckoned by the *Doing Business* studies of the IFC/World Bank study to have the best business climate among major Indian cities. However, too much should not be read into this—the correct interpretation is that Punjab is less of a laggard than other states, but far behind places elsewhere in the world. India ranks just 134th out of 183 countries in ease of doing business, so being India's best does not mean excellence by international standards.[5]

Some Myths about Punjab's Decline

Why has Punjab suffered relative decline in the last two decades? Politicians and academics in Punjab reel out a long list of reasons but most of these turn out to be exaggerated or downright false.

Myth No. 1: India has fought several wars with Pakistan across the Punjab border and fears of fresh wars have kept industry away from Punjab

Normally, successful agriculture produces lots of consuming power for farmers and workers, and becomes a good basis for industrialisation. Punjab also has a good road network and is not too far from the major metropolis of Delhi. The state's scholars claim that industrialisation has been held back by the fact that it is a border state, next door to Pakistan, with whom India has fought three full-scale wars and several other skirmishes. Because of this, they say, New Delhi has been reluctant to allow major investments in the state, since these would be sitting ducks for Pakistani aircraft in the event of a war. This, they claim, has artificially held back the state's industrialisation and hence its GDP growth.[6]

The claim is manifestly false. Gujarat is also a border state with Pakistan, and is the most industrialised and fastest-growing state in India. Even Rajasthan, another border state that is backward and mostly desert, seriously lacking infrastructure and agricultural potential, has grown faster than Punjab (see Table 2.1). It is worth mentioning that the original Punjab state was in 1965 split into two, with the most backward southern part forming a new state, Haryana. This once-backward portion now grows much faster than the once-advanced portion that is still called Punjab. To be fair, Haryana has a special advantage that other states don't—it surrounds Delhi state on three sides, so Delhi's urban sprawl has spilled over into Haryana.

There was indeed a time, in the 1960s and 1970s, when the central government sometimes seemed hesitant to build major public sector industrial projects in Punjab because of its location next to Pakistan. Nevertheless, it built a railway coach factory at Kapurthala, a unit of Hindustan Machine Tools in Ludhiana, and helped launch Punjab Tractors in Mohali. There have been no hostilities across India's western border with Pakistan (comprising the states of Punjab, Rajasthan and Gujarat) since 1971. In none of the three Indo-Pak wars of 1947, 1965 and 1971 was there bombing by either side of industrial factories—the focus was on military targets.

In any case the public sector has long ceased to be the driving force of industry in India and economic reform starting in the 1980s and accelerating in the 1990s have put the private sector in the driver's seat. The private sector has invested massively in two other border states, Gujarat and Rajasthan, but much less in Punjab. Clearly proximity to Pakistan is not a good excuse for Punjab's slippage in the economic growth table.

New Delhi has permitted Reliance Industries Ltd to put up the largest oil refinery complex in the world in Gujarat, within easy reach of Pakistan's Air Force. Essar Oil has built the country's second biggest refinery complex in the same state. This year, a joint venture of Hindustan Petroleum Corporation Ltd. (a central government-owned company) and Mittal Industries has commissioned a big 9-million tonne oil refinery at Bathinda in Punjab, just 100 kilometers from the Pakistan border. This disproves the thesis that New Delhi's war paranoia has held up industrial projects in Punjab. Indeed, the Bathinda refinery may soon export fuel to Pakistan.[7]

New Delhi has built an international airport at Amritsar, a stone-throw away from the Pakistan border. The state's politicians claim that this international airport has not been allowed to develop because it is just a few miles from the border. The claim is not convincing—if indeed security were such an important consideration, surely New Delhi would never have created an international airport at Amritsar in the first place.

Myth No 2: Sikh terrorism caused Punjab's decline

Sikh militant separatists wanting to create an independent state of Khalistan were on the rampage in Punjab from the start of the 1980s to 1993. The state at one point became so ungovernable that it was placed under martial law. During the insurrection, New Delhi sought some sort of accommodation with disgruntled Sikhs, but failed dismally. Martial law also failed. Then in the 1990s a new Congress government came to power and decided to crack down on militants, using the police, not the army. The police had the local knowledge needed to hunt down the militants, and used some of the same savage tactics that the militants themselves had used. Although this implied major violations of civil rights, it succeeded in finally crushing Sikh militancy by 1993.

Now, it is true that in the heyday of Sikh militancy in the 1980s, industrialists were not keen on opening new factories in the state. Some industries that were located in Punjab (such as Hero Honda, India's biggest motor-cycle manufacturer) built new factories in other states. But Sikh terrorism ended two decades ago, and Punjab's decline has continued nevertheless. Prof Gurmail Singh of Punjab University points out that Sikh militants had a complete grip of western districts but not of eastern districts of the states, yet industrial growth from the 1980s onwards was weak in both eastern and western districts.[8]

Today, many Indian states face Maoist insurrections, which sometimes look as threatening as Sikh militancy once was in Punjab. In the last decade, an estimated 167 out of 600 Indian districts have suffered from some form of Maoist violence. Yet this violence has not come in the way of India achieving its fastest growth in history. The most entrenched Maoist-held areas are in the state of Chhattisgarh, which has huge forests, relatively few roads, and limited administrative breadth. The Maoists control very large areas in the state. Yet Chhattisgarh has been in the last decade one of India's fastest growing states, averaging 9.1 per cent per year between 2002-03 and 2010-11 (see Table 2.1). It is a major producer of steel, sponge iron and aluminum. No doubt it has the advantage of big mineral deposits but Maoists have seriously disrupted this. The contrast between economic growth in Punjab and Chhattisgarh demonstrates that terrorism does not necessarily mean economic decline, and can coexist with double-digit growth. Besides, almost two decades have passed since the end of terrorism in Punjab, so it is a poor excuse for the state's continuing weak performance.

Punjab politicians say that the state accumulated huge debts because of low revenues and the high cost of combating terrorism in the terrorist era, and claim that New Delhi has not given enough debt relief to Punjab to get rid of this historical burden. In her 2011-12 budget speech, the Punjab Finance Minister Ms Upinder Kaur said, "Punjab was a revenue surplus State until 1986-87 and its debt burden was only 27 per cent of Gross State Domestic Product. By 1994-95 the debt rose almost to 36 per cent of Gross State Domestic Product owing to successive revenue and fiscal deficits in these eight years. These were the years of militancy in Punjab and the State was under a long spell of President's Rule from 1987 to 1992. The Central Government, which was then running the administration of the State, followed a policy of high non-productive expenditure without raising any resources and to achieve this, it plugged the gap with unproductive and often high-cost loans. The debt burden of the State is a legacy of militancy, long years of President's Rule and an indiscriminate fiscal policy followed by the Central Government."[9]

This is disputed strongly by New Delhi. A former Finance Ministry official who dealt with Punjab's debt problems says that debt relief for the terrorist era has been given in ample measure by the Twelfth and Thirteenth Finance Commissions (these commissions periodically decide on how central government revenues should be shared with the states and what allowances are required for the special conditions in some states). The real problem, says the official, is that slow GDP growth has meant slow revenue growth and its fiscal impact has been compounded by huge non-productive subsidies, mainly for electricity. The official adds that most Punjab politicians got used to having several personal security staff in their entourage during the terrorism era of 1980-1992 and are reluctant to give these up. Punjab has a very high police/population ratio but the police are diverted massively from standard law and order operations to VIP security. This is a huge waste of public funds.[10]

Myth No 3: Punjab is very distant from the sea and so is unable to grow as fast as states with ports

No doubt coastal locations have their advantages. No doubt closeness to a port helps develop export industries. Yet Punjab was just as far from the sea through most of its history, including the first three decades after Indian independence and this did not prevent it from becoming one of India's richest, fastest-growing states. The world over, land-locked states complain that they are seriously disadvantaged, yet many of them grow fast. In South Asia, Bhutan has been the fastest-growing country and has comfortably overtaken India in per capita income. In Africa, land-locked Botswana has overtaken coastal South Africa to become the continent's richest country. After the collapse of communism in the Soviet Union and Eastern Europe, the richest of the ex-communist states has turned out to be Slovenia, which is virtually land-locked (it has only one minor port and exports mainly through Trieste in Italy).[11]

The lesson is clear. Geography is not destiny. Land-locked areas may have disadvantages but are capable of becoming rich and fast-growing if they follow the right policies. Just as badly land-locked as Punjab are the two neighbouring hill states of Himachal Pradesh and Uttarakhand, both of whom have grown much faster than Punjab (see Table 2.1). However, these two states have been aided by tax breaks bestowed by New Delhi.

Until the 1980s, New Delhi followed a "freight equalisation policy" that enabled all states to get industrial inputs like coal and steel at the same government-ordained price. Once freight equalisation was abandoned in the 1990s, Punjab's distance from coal mines and steel plants became a disadvantage. However, many other states were just as disadvantaged in distance from coal mines and steel plants but fared well. The best example of this was Gujarat, which became India's fastest-growing major state even as Punjab kept slipping (see Table 2.1).

Myth No 4: Punjab has no metallic minerals or coal and so loses out to states that do

Punjab suffers from chronic power shortages and this has been an important discouraging factor for potential industrialists. Indian coal has a high rock content, so transporting coal from coalfields—all of which are very distant—means transporting almost as much rock as coal, thus raising generating costs. The main mineral-bearing areas are in central and eastern India. Punjab's politicians claim that a lack of raw materials has placed the state at a serous disadvantage.

However, the mineral-rich central and eastern states have historically been among India's most backward and slow-growing. This is because minerals in India are generally found in mountainous jungle areas with few roads or other infrastructure, inhabited by tribes with some of the highest poverty, lowest literacy and worst health indicators in India. The mountainous terrain makes road and railway building difficult and expensive. Through history, across the globe, vibrant agriculture has been the driver of growth in rich civilisations, not minerals. That has always been true of India as a whole.

One reason for this is that minerals should not be interpreted to be just coal or metallic ores. Good agricultural soil is a form of mineral wealth and this was the driver of all great ancient civilisations from Egypt to China. And Punjab has this sort of mineral wealth in abundance—its soils are excellent for agriculture and rank among the best in India. This is one reason why its agricultural yields are the highest among any state.

Mineral wealth is by no means a key determinant of either industrialisation or GDP. Maharashtra, Tamil Nadu and Gujarat are India's most industrialised states, with high GDPs. None of them has major minerals. Maharashtra has substantial coal reserves for power generation but Gujarat and Tamil Nadu do not. Looking across the globe, we find that countries like Japan, Korea and now China have shown it is possible to import minerals from across the world and yet produce internationally competitive industries and become miracle economies. Punjab itself was the fifth-most industrialised state in India in the 1980s, despite the lack of nearby minerals or coal. The reasons for its subsequent decline have to be found elsewhere.

The Real Reasons for Punjab's Relative Decline

Punjab's relative decline can be traced to several factors, of which the most important is a serious fiscal crunch. This in turn is due mainly to the supply of free electricity to farmers. Other reasons include the agricultural plateau reached by the green revolution; the failure to diversify fast enough out of agriculture; the failure to make the educational investments necessary to induce a switch to service industries like computer software; very high land prices that have discouraged industry; and Central Government tax breaks for neighouring hill states that led to an unwarranted flight of industry from Punjab to these states.

The fiscal crunch

Punjab used to have large revenue surpluses in its glory days in the 1960s and 1970s. But in recent decades it has persistently run a high fiscal deficit, which is currently the highest among all major states (budgeted at 3.8% of GDP for 2011-12). This high figure arises mainly out of huge unwarranted subsidies, the chief culprit being free power to farmers. One consequence is that the government is not even able to pay all salaries on time. This leads to demoralisation and cynicism among staff, who look for avenues to make money illegally.

Like other states, Punjab has enacted a Fiscal Responsibility and Budget Management Act, which aims to reduce the state's revenue deficit to zero (that is, borrowing will be used only for capital spending, not current expenditure). In fact the revenue deficit has increased from 1.8 per cent of GDP in 2011-12 to 2.75 per cent in 2011-12. The state has often argued that it ran into huge revenue losses in the period 1986-1992 when Sikh terrorists launched a major insurrection. However, as noted in the previous section of this chapter, the state has been given debt relief by three Finance Commissions in a row and besides terrorism ended two decades ago. So this excuse wears very thin. The major problem lies in runaway subsidies, above all the supply of free electricity to rural areas.

The original composite Punjab state was split into Haryana and a truncated Punjab in 1965. Haryana was at the time regarded as the most backward part of the original state, yet it has forged ahead and boasts strong revenue growth and a surplus on current budget account, in contrast to Punjab's weak finances. Some Punjab academics say the state's tax administration is weak because of high levels of corruption.[12]

In his speech presenting the Punjab budget for 2012-13, Finance Minister Dhindsa said, "The actual revenue deficit for 2011-12 has shot up to ₹ 6,838 crore ($1,368 million) against ₹ 3,379 crore ($676 million) in the Budget estimates. The slippage in the target is mainly on account of no additional resource mobilisation measures and increase in salary and pensions." The minister further said "the committed expenditure on account of salaries, pensions, interest payments and power subsidy is likely to be ₹ 30,560 crore ($6,130 million) in 2012-13—amounting to 80.44 per cent of the revenue receipts of the year. The level of debt is also not sustainable. The gross borrowings for 2012-13 will be ₹ 13,204 crore ($2,641 million), which will mainly go into repaying the principal amount and interest, leaving only ₹ 2,936 crore ($587 million) in the hands of the state. More than 80 per cent of the net borrowings are going into meeting revenue deficit, leaving only 20 per cent for capital expenditure. The interest payments as percentage of revenue receipts have increased to 23.5 per cent in 2011-12—this is one of the highest for any state in the country."[13]

The ruling coalition of the Akali Dal and Bharatiya Janata Party has also resorted to other subsidies to win votes. These include subsidised *atta* (wheat flour) and dal (lentils and gram), free bicycles to all school children, and a marriage grant (*shagun*) to new brides. Punjab is hardly alone in distributing freebies. Other states like Tamil Nadu have given voters colour TVs and laptops. Yet these other states are able to generate a revenue surplus, while Punjab cannot. The main problem is its exceptionally high burden arising from free electricity.[14]

The curse of free rural electricity

Competition between political parties for farmers' votes has led over the years to electricity being supplied by the Punjab government to farmers free of charge since 1998. Canal water is also virtually free in canal-irrigated areas. At one time, subsidised electricity was seen as a way of promoting the green revolution, which required assured irrigation. But, as Ashok Gulati says in a separate chapter in this report, "since demand for such subsidised inputs greatly exceeds the supply, the quantity farmers get is rationed by government agencies. Rationing limits the number of connections, hours of electricity supplied, and days on which canal water is released into canals. Where states charge for electricity, it is generally as a flat monthly rate per horse-power, with no meters. The marginal cost of pumping becomes zero. This induces farmers to growing inappropriate water-intensive and electricity-intensive crops such as paddy and sugarcane even in low-rainfall areas. For example, paddy in Punjab and Haryana requires roughly 225 centimeters of irrigation water per crop. But the annual rainfall is only 60 centimetres. So, farmers have to pump huge amounts of ground water for thirsty paddy, depleting the water table at an alarming rate (33 cms per year, according to NASA satellites during 2002-2008)."

Apart from this destruction of acquifers, free farm electricity has now become the biggest cause of the state's fiscal troubles. S.S. Johl, former head of Punjab Agricultural University, says that the state's total debt is ₹ 78,000 crore ($15.6 billion) and contingent liabilities through guarantees are another ₹ 40,000 crores ($8 billion). He estimates that 90 per cent of this debt burden has arisen from the enormous cumulative impact of electricity subsidies, currently running at over ₹ 5,000 crore per year. He says one of the consequences of the fiscal crisis is that salary payments are delayed by months in most government departments and also in Punjab Agricultural University.

Johl says that, when he was advisor to former Chief Minister Amarinder Singh, he negotiated a loan of ₹ 1,000 crore ($200 million) from the World Bank for revamping the state's marketing systems and run-down power transmission system. But this was tied to reforms, including the reduction of power subsidies. Initially, the state government was willing to limit free electricity to small farms but as the next state election drew close, the government made electricity free for all farmers, abandoning all pretense of reform. The World Bank refused to proceed with the loan, so the state lost a badly-needed project.

Johl says that the so-called subsidy to farmers is actually passed on to consumers, and so does not benefit farmers at all. The Commission on Agricultural Costs and Prices determines the minimum support price for different crops every year based on actual input costs. The subsidy on rural electricity leads to a correspondingly lower support price. This benefits consumers of grain, not farmers. Yet Punjab's political parties find it politically impossible to charge farmers.

Some farmers have huge holdings and up to 150 tubewells each, says Johl, so the rich are benefiting disproportionately from the subsidy. He estimates that 83 per cent of farms are smaller than 2 hectares (5 acres). These small farmers initially installed centrifugal pumps costing around ₹ 30,000 ($600). But these stopped working when the water table fell. Farmers now have to install submersible wells costing up to ₹ 200,000 ($4,000) and only better-off farmers can afford this. They in turn cream off the bulk of the subsidy. And they are mainly responsible for the calamitous fall in the water table. This needs to be combated by a switch to sprinkler irrigation and drip irrigation, both of which conserve use of water. But this switch will not be possible till farmers have to pay for water and so have an incentive to use water-saving technologies.

Meanwhile fiscal strain means the state government has been unable to build any new power plants for several years. In the early 1980s, says Johl, Punjab spent up to 60 per cent of its budget on increasing power generation and transmission, and this helped drive the state's growth. Those days are over. The state's transmission and distribution (T&D) system is in terrible shape and badly needs rehabilitation and upgradation to cut transmission losses. Acute power shortages have discouraged new industries from investing in the state.

Thus, the political decision to subsidise farm electricity has become an unwitting tax on industry and has hobbled the state's development

Punjab is now trying to overcome the problem by asking private sector companies to generate power (historically, power generation, T&D was a state monopoly). Several new private sector power plants are expected to be commissioned in the next two years. The state will soon get 1,940 mw from Vedanta (at Talwandi Sabo), 1,400 mw from L&T (at Rajpura) and 540 mw from GVK (at Goindwal). This should improve the very tardy pace of industrialisation. But experience in other states shows that bankrupt state governments tend to renege on deals with private power generators and so convert ostensibly profitable power projects into unprofitable ones. Many states have refused to allow tariff increases to compensate for higher fuel costs and many are in arrears of payment to private suppliers for the electricity they buy in order to distribute free to farmers. The electricity outlook remains clouded.[15]

The green revolution tapers off

Punjab pioneered the green revolution in India through the use of high yielding seeds, accompanied by high doses of fertiliser and water. Punjab Agricultural University (PAU) modified high-yielding seeds from Mexico and other sources to suit Punjab's agroclimatic conditions. However, by the 1990s, gains from the new dwarf varieties of rice and wheat introduced in the 1960s had mostly worn off. PAU, which had developed the first seeds for the green revolution, has failed to keep up the good work by creating ever-better varieties. Its researchers are demoralised by the state's priorities of wooing farmers and other with massive subsidies, leaving the state government with insufficient money to pay salaries on time, or to fill vacant posts. S.S. Johl says that politicians criticise PAU for not producing enough new high-yielding varieties in recent years but how can demoralised researchers without salaries be expected to produce research breakthroughs? Many good scientists have left for greener pastures.

Private sector agricultural research cannot make good this gap in full. Private seed companies can and have produced excellent new varieties of hybrid maize and genetically modified cotton, because for such crops farmers have to buy seeds afresh from the companies every year and the companies can thus recover their research costs with a profit. But in the case of self-pollinating crops like wheat and rice, farmers can simply save grains from the last harvest and use these as seeds for the next season, without buying seeds afresh from companies. Companies will not do any research for such crops because they have no way of recovering their research costs. For such crops, public sector research is inescapable. PAU used to be at the very fore of R&D in self-pollinating crops like rice and wheat and its decline has therefore affected the growth of agricultural productivity in the state.

Fast-expanding tubewell irrigation was initially the driving force of agricultural growth, but once 95 per cent of the land had come under irrigation, this ceased to be a source of dynamism. Excessive tubewell pumping, perversely encouraged by the supply of free electricity to farmers, has in some districts exhausted sweet ground water but farmers started pumping the brackish water underneath. This led to salt deposition on the soil, rendering some areas infertile.[16]

The state government also had a historically efficient network of canals but land along these canals has tended to get waterlogged and saline, because of imperfect drainage. The supply of virtually free canal water has deprived the state of revenue to maintain canals and ensure proper drainage. Large areas need reclamation with chemicals to restore yields, and one such reclamation project has been done at Kandi in Hoshiarpur district with World Bank assistance. Watershed development was actively followed in earlier decades in the hilly areas of the state to conserve water. But now most of the tanks and reservoirs built in the watersheds have silted up and have not been restored. The problem is that these tanks belong to and are operated by the state government. Had they been handed over to local communities, they might have fared better.[17]

The state attempted after the 1980s to diversify into fruit and vegetables. But the shift was never fast enough and constant power cuts in rural areas meant that good cold chains—essential for preserving fruit and vegetables—were not possible. The central government limited active procurement at guaranteed support prices to rice and wheat and farmers were therefore reluctant to shift to other crops whose prices were far more volatile. The state did indeed develop a vibrant dairy industry. *Basmati* rice has a much lower yield than high-yielding dwarf varieties but fetches a premium price. However, the bulk of the state's farm area continues with an ecologically destructive rotation of high-yielding wheat and rice, which has lowered the water table disastrously. Traditional drinking water wells have all run dry because of this. Many shallower tubewells of small farmers have also run dry as the water table keeps falling. Of the state's 127 development blocks (this is an administrative unit), no less than 105 are now called "dark areas" where the fall in the water table is completely unsustainable. In some areas the sweet water is all gone and only brackish water remains. This has affected the state's agricultural dynamism.

Failures in agricultural marketing

Punjab, like most other Indian states, has an Agricultural Produce Marketing Committee Act that makes it mandatory for farmers to sell most sorts of agricultural produce only in government-organised markets called *mandis*. The Act was supposed to protect farmers from exploitation by private traders offering throwaway prices. The state government itself procured major crops like wheat and paddy at specified minimum support prices. However, there is in practice no government procurement of other crops at specified support prices. In the case of these other crops, the *mandis* have obtained a trade monopoly that is mercilessly exploited by a limited group of traders with political connections. Former Chief Secretary S.C. Aggarwal says that many bureaucrats have attempted to end the monopoly of *mandis* but met with severe political resistance—traders are prominent politicians and are also traditional financiers of leading political parties. The state government extracts almost 14.5 per cent in various levies from the *mandis* and this is a major source of revenue.

Traditionally, the grain procurement agencies of the central and state governments made payments to the big middlemen at the *mandis*, who then paid farmers with a lag. This often led to disputes and heartburn among farmers. However, with the rapid spread of cellphones into rural areas, it is now feasible to get farmers to open bank accounts and get payments online directly into their accounts. New Delhi has asked all states to try and make payments directly to farmers if possible, and this has been adopted by some states, including historically backward ones like Madhya Pradesh. But Punjab has not done so despite having one of the highest rates of rural cellphone penetration. It still makes payments through the big traders, once again underlining their political clout.

Many private sector corporations would like to buy produce directly from farmers—this will eliminate layers of middlemen and prove a win-

win for both farmers and consumers. But trading interests have been able to sabotage this move. Ashok Gulati writes in a separate chapter in this volume, "Crops like fruits and vegetables need to be freed from marketing controls ordained by obsolete APMC (Agricultural Produce Marketing Committee) laws. Indeed, the APMC Act needs to be changed to encourage direct sourcing by retailers from farmers' groups, to compress supply chains by removing unnecessary middlemen, and to invest in back-end infrastructure. For this organised retailers, both domestic and foreign, need to be encouraged and incentivised."

Failure to catch the services revolution

When Punjab was among the very forefront of states in the 1970s, it had every opportunity to prepare for a switch out of agriculture into industry and services. It was already among India's foremost states in roads, rural electrification and per capita income, and could have invested in education to produce the skills needed for further economic development. The Central government had in 1963 set up one of its prestigious Indian Institutes of Technology (IIT) at Ropar in Punjab. Now, such IITs helped spark the computer software revolution in Bangalore, Mumbai and several other Indian cities. But not in Punjab.

One reason for the state's neglect of higher education and information technology was that its politicians never evolved from a mind-set that emphasised agriculture above all else, and focused on buying the votes of farmers through subsidies rather than diversification out of agriculture. Punjab did indeed compete with other states in trying to attract industry but hardly at all in trying to attract high-tech services. So Punjab was left far behind the states in southern and western India that spearheaded the IT revolution.[18]

In 1965, the current Punjab state was carved out of the composite historical one as a Sikh-majority state which would institute Punjabi in the Gurmukhi script (used by traditional Sikhs) as the state's official language. This religion-based emphasis on promoting Punjabi meant that the state educational system had insufficient interest in pushing for English language education. Other states saw that good English skills were vital to reap the benefits of globalisation, most obviously in the form of business outsourcing and call centres. The Punjab government failed to emphasise English for so long in government schools that desperate parents started sending their children to private schools that cost more than free government schools but taught English.[19]

Free electricity and the consequent fiscal crunch have seriously impeded growth of public spending on education and health, which has historically been below levels in other Asian developing countries (see Table 2.2). Despite this low base, such spending has grown more slowly in Punjab than in almost any other state in recent times. In public education, Punjab's average growth rate was just 7.7 per cent per year in 2004-2010 against the national average of 14.9 per cent, and 21.2 per cent in Haryana, which used to be the backward portion of the original composite Punjab. In health, Punjab's growth was just 5.5 per cent per year against the national average of 14.4 per cent and Haryana's 28.4 per cent. Adjusted for inflation, there was hardly any real growth at all in Punjab's social spending. This neglect of education is one reason why Punjab has failed to climb onto the services bandwagon that most other advanced Indian states managed to do.[20]

TABLE 2.2

Growth of Public Spending on Education and Health (% per year, 2004-2010)

	Public Education	*Public Health*
Andhra Pradesh	12.1	14.3
Assam	9.1	25.7
Bihar	16.7	22.4
Chhattisgarh	20.6	17.2
Gujarat	10.6	10.9
Haryana	21.2	28.4
Jharkhand	21.4	18.4
Karnataka	14.6	12.1
Kerala	12.2	19.8
Madhya Pradesh	13.2	11.5
Maharashtra	13.4	13.2
Orissa	17.2	11.2
Punjab	7.7	5.5
Rajasthan	14.0	21.6
Tamil Nadu	15.6	10.8
Uttar Pradesh	19.8	12.4
West Bengal	10.7	5.1
All India	14.9	14.4

Source: Rao, M. Govinda (2012). *States' Fiscal Development and Implications for Regional Development*. National Institute of Public Finance and Policy. August.

Prof Gurmail Singh complains almost half the posts of teachers in government have not filled because of the fiscal crisis: retirees are simply not replaced. Many teachers have not been paid for months. Teacher absenteeism is high in all Indian states but Bihar and Punjab are the two worst. The quality of teaching was poor even in earlier times when salaries were paid regularly but non-payment would have further reduced whatever incentive there was to teach properly.

The Tribune, Chandigarh, reported in February 2012 that 840 headmasters were not receiving their salaries. Of 500 senior teachers recently promoted to the rank of headmaster, 380 were not receiving their salaries and so were regretting their promotion. The situation is as bad in medical colleges and health centres. Prof Surinder Shukla of Panjab University says she went to Muktsar district to study teacher absenteeism in schools. She was surprised to find that most teachers were totally disillusioned and demoralised. Interestingly, the majority of them were looking for ways to migrate to jobs abroad. Punjabis have always been globe-trotters, and the state even has a TV channel devoted to emmigration and allied issues.

The curse of high land prices

Prosperous rural areas have high land prices and it is natural for Punjab land to be expensive. It is also natural that Punjabis going overseas have for decades sent remittances home and these have typically been used by families to keep buying more land, pushing up prices. However, land prices in Punjab (and indeed in most Indian states) have been artificially inflated by perverse tax and administrative laws. Unlike other assets, farmland is exempted from capital gains tax and this distortion attracts a flood of money. Moreover, buying land is a hassle- free way of laundering black money in India. Because of high stamp duty, rural land is typically registered at a tiny fraction of the contract price in order to reduce stamp duty payment. Often half or more is paid in cash under the table and this means that black money can easily be laundered into respectable land. Such money laundering has sent land prices skyrocketing everywhere in India but the rates are highest in areas with flat fertile land, as in Punjab. This is good for land speculators but bad news for industries that need large parcels of land. Other states have plenty of relatively cheap rocky land and barren land that can be offered to industries to set up factories. But Punjab has very little such land and so is unable to provide land cheaply for industry.

Corporations are used to demanding and getting land very cheaply from state governments, which typically acquire land, using their power of eminent domain and then sell or lease this land at a highly subsidised rate to industries. Punjab has not only high land prices but also serious fiscal problems, which limit its ability to subsidise land for industry. S.C. Aggarwal, former Chief Secretary of Punjab, says that the Tata group initially wanted to set up its plant for its famous Nano car—billed as the cheapest car in the world at $2,500—in Punjab. But Tata wanted lots of cheap land for its factory and ancillary suppliers, plus tax breaks and Punjab could not afford to provide this. Aggarwal calculates that the net present value of tax breaks and cheap land demanded by the Tata group would have been ₹ 1,200 crore ($240 million), whereas Tata's own investment was just ₹ 700 crore ($140 million). Tata looked elsewhere, got excellent terms from the Gujarat government and located its plant there. Again, Reliance Industries Ltd was very keen on establishing a large food retail chain in Punjab, procuring produce directly from farmers. But Reliance wanted a lot of cheap land for warehousing and the state found it impossible to meet this demand, so Reliance went to other states.

In one case, says Aggarwal, the state had to pay one crore rupees ($200,000) per acre for acquiring land near Mohali for a technology park. No industry was likely to buy land at this rate but high-tech industries (including information technology companies) would find it possible. Even in deep rural areas, the price of land is ₹ 50 lakh ($100,000) per acre, too costly to attract most industries.

Flight of capital to neighbouring states getting tax breaks

Punjab complains that tax breaks given by New Delhi to industrial units in the nearby hill states of Himachal Pradesh and Uttarakhand have resulted in a flight of industry out of Punjab into the hill states. In 2003, New Delhi announced a special scheme of exemption from excise duty for units established in hilly states, including Himachal Pradesh and Uttarakhand, which adjoin Punjab. This created an industrial boom in both hill states—major industrial groups including Tata, Bajaj, Nestle, Mahindra, Hindustan Unilever, Britannia and LG set up new units to take advantage of this tax benefit. Any unit starting production between 2003 and 2010 was guaranteed excise duty exemption for 10 years after starting production. The implicit subsidy (foregone tax revenue) to industrial units has been estimated at over ₹ 10,000 crore ($2 billion) per year. Several Punjab industrialists set up new units in these states rather than expand in Punjab itself.

This preferential tax break was unwarranted. It was ostensibly aimed to offset the difficulties of establishing industries in hilly regions. Yet the industries that actually came up were in the narrow plains regions of these states, not the hilly areas. Punjab can fairly argue that the tax breaks diverted some Punjabi capital to these hill states. But the biggest investors in these states came from the western and southern India, and industrial growth in those two regions was not adversely affected at all. This factor alone cannot explain Punjab's slow rate of industrialisation. That is better explained by chronic power shortages, neglect of higher education, high land prices, corruption and fiscal problems. Punjab's investment rate used to be above the national average but has fallen below it since the 1990s. Prof Ranjit Ghuman of CRRID, Chandigarh, estimates that the state would have received an additional ₹ 9,500 crore ($1.9 billion) of investment had it simply matched the national investment average between 1995-96 and 2008-09.[21]

Some industry is nevertheless coming up. The 6 million tonne oil refinery at Bathinda is the biggest new unit and it could add a big chemical unit. New power plants built by the private sector will soon reduce the chronic power shortage. A pharmaceuticals cluster has come up at Mohali. Several companies have built or expanded factories for tractors, combine harvesters and other farm machinery. Abhishek Industries has put up a big mill making paper from agricultural waste. Nevertheless, Punjab remains an industrial under-performer.

Lack of trade with Pakistan

In the 1970s, Indian policy aimed at self-sufficiency and discouraged foreign trade. That robbed India's coastal states of an important locational advantage but did not affect Punjab. To that extent, Punjab gained relative to other states. But when the economy was liberalised in 1991, the coastal states boomed, with flourishing exports and imports. Punjab was unable to register similar gains because it was far away from any port. However, being land-locked and far from the sea is not necessarily fatal. For instance Austria and Switzerland are land-locked but are prosperous trading economies. This is because[22] they have excellent road and rail connections with neighbouring European states, with whom they share a free trade zone. By contrast, trade between India and Pakistan has been blocked or banned since the war of 1965 and existing trade is limited to relatively few items. This has deprived Punjab of the usual gains of international trade.

India has long offered Pakistan Most Favoured Nation (MFN) treatment under WTO rules but its non-tariff barriers (NTB) remain substantial. Pakistan has long refused to offer India MFN status, saying there could be no normalisation of trade or commercial relations until the Kashmir dispute between the two countries was settled. Only a limited number of Indian items were listed for import by Pakistan. Much of what was traded went by sea, not across the Punjab land border. There is still no provision for trucks and railway wagons to pass seamlessly from one country into the other. One consequence has been that South Asia is one of the world's least integrated regions in trade. The world over, regional trading agreements have facilitated rapid economic growth. But war, terrorism and political suspicion have prevented this from happening in South Asia. This has been especially detrimental to Punjab.[23]

However, recently Indo-Pak relations have shown signs of improvement, and Pakistan has indicated that it wishes to normalise trade relations. India has welcomed the change. This is a dramatic development, even though the process will probably be gradual. Till now, Pakistan has had a list of only 2,000 items that can be imported from India and of these only 137 could be imported through the land border with Punjab—the rest had to go by sea. This is to be replaced by a Pakistani negative list of 1,123 items (which cannot be imported) and this allows more than 7,0000 items to be imported from India. India has asked Pakistan to permit all these items to go through the land border. Too much not be expected quickly. But it means that Punjab's trade and economic prospects will brighten considerably. Already there is talk of expanding the HPCL-Mittal oil refinery from 6 million tonnes to 9 million tonnes to meet Pakistani demand for petroleum products like gasoline and to build a pipeline to Pakistan to transport the products.

Instead of being a deeply land-locked state with poor international trade prospects, Punjab could become the major Indian gateway to Pakistan. Most Indo-Pak trade currently goes by sea to the port of Karachi. But 55 per cent of Pakistan's population is in the Pakistani state of Punjab, a long way from Karachi but just across the border from Indian Punjab. So, Indian Punjab is well placed not only to become a supply base for Indian exports but as the gateway for Pakistan goods to enter India.

Some Positive Trends

The opening of trade with Pakistan is not by any means the only positive item in Punjab's future outlook. There are other bright spots too.

First, the tax breaks for Himachal Pradesh and Uttarakhand have ended in 2010. Even though reports of capital flight from Punjab to these states were exaggerated, whatever flight did occur has now ended.

Second, the fiscal crisis in the state has obliged ruling politicians to find finances outside the budget to finance essential infrastructure and services. So it has gone for public-private partnerships (PPPs) in a big way in areas that were formerly government monopolies. Electricity, roads, bridges, hospitals, schools, bus transport and other areas once reserved for the government have now been opened to PPPs or outright private investment. This promises to ease infrastructural bottlenecks, especially in electricity, with five new private sector power plants coming up. This will end the crippling power shortages that have long discouraged industrial investment in the state. The quality of hospitals, buses, schools and colleges is also expected to improve with private sector participation. The PPP model had also brought in new sources of revenue, for instance from fees paid by private bus operators on routes that were once government monopolies.[24]

However, PPPs in all states have been afflicted with allegations of corruption, and Punjab is no exception. Several bus routes and bus categories (like luxury buses) have been monopolised by a cartel of companies widely believed to be owned by politicians. If any independent operator attempts to enter the fray and break the cartel, he is physically threatened, and gets no protection from the state. Most private sector bus licences have been given for air-conditioned and luxury buses. The Tribune, a leading state newspaper, complains that the tax on conditioned buses has been halved, and on luxury buses has been cut from ₹ 7.50 ($0.15) to just ₹ 0.50 ($0.01) per km. This represents the worst sort of crony capitalism. Yet, at the end of it all, bus services have greatly expanded in quality and quantity, and government revenue from transport has also risen. The shift in service provision from the public sector to the private sector, warts and all, has produced major gains.

Third, the state set up an Administrative Reforms Commission in 2008, and some of the recommended reforms have been implemented. They promise a big improvement in governance.[25] The first phase of the reforms included a Right to Service Act that empowers citizens to demand and get better services from a corrupt, slothful bureaucracy. Implementation of this is spotty. But to a fair extent, citizens have been empowered to demand and get various services and certificate without the usual delays and bribes. Ration cards for subsidised food now have to be issued within 6 days of application. Citizens can complain against the police for non-action on grievances. The need for affidavits and other documents has been reduced. The ruling Akali Dal-BJP coalition government believes that the Right to Service was an important reason for its election victory in 2012. It has now launched the second phase of administrative in August 2012, with further measures to make the police and bureaucracy accountable to citizens through grievance redressal procedures.[26]

Fourth, the state has become one of the first to overhaul obsolete land policies to freely allow and record long-term leases. It has not placed any time limit on leases, leaving this to be decided mutually by owners and lessors. Since independence, all state governments have sought to discourage tenancy and emphasise "land-to-the-tiller" policies. This might have made sense when feudal lords owned huge areas of land. But today four-fifths of operational holdings are less than two hectares and land fragmentation is worsening as each plot is divided among several children after the death of a father. Once, rich farmers leased in land from poor ones. The opposite is happening now as rich farmers leave for cities and lease out their land to small farmers. But most leasing is informal and unrecorded—the owners are paranoid about losing their land to the tenant if there is any official tenancy record. However, the Punjab government says it will legalise long-term land leases. Many such reforms run into problems in practice but the Confederation of Indian Industry (CII) has hailed Punjab's initiative. Long-term leases will encourage lessors to make investments in the land. Such leases will encourage the consolidation of tiny plots into large economic farms and may usher in a new era of corporate farming.[27]

Fifth, despite problems like high land prices and power shortages, Punjab is widely viewed as a state that is investor-friendly, and encourages industry. As mentioned in the introductory section, Ludhiana, the biggest and most industrialised city in the state, is reckoned by the *Doing Business* studies of the IFC/World Bank study to have the best business climate among major Indian cities. It is worth looking at the study in some detail, as this is among the few sources of comparative data across states.[28]

Ludhiana, Punjab, is India's best city for ease of doing business

The IFC/World Bank produces an annual report on *Doing Business*, comparing countries across the world. India fares very poorly in these reports. In its 2012 report, India ranked a lowly 132nd of 183 countries in overall ease of doing business. In ease of starting a new business, India was even worse—it came 166th. In ease of getting a construction permit —a prime area of corruption—India was 181st, or third last in the world. In enforcement of contract—something supposedly essential for any business—India came 182nd, or second last! So, for all the economic liberalisation since 1991, much remains to be done. Most of these hurdles are at the state government and municipal level: these are the levels in charge of registration of new businesses, construction permits and the police-legal system. The states have clearly lagged well behind New Delhi in embracing economic reform.

The *Doing Business* series does not compare different states of India. But in 2009, it produced a special study called *Doing Business in India* which compared the business environment in different cities of India. This gives a fair idea of business conditions in the 17 major states.

Of the 17 cities it examined, top position went to Ludhiana, Punjab. There is no reason to think that conditions are worse in other Punjab cities. It appears that, among Indian cities, Punjab has created one of the most business-friendly environments. This does not mean, of course, that Ludhiana is particularly good compared with cities in other countries.

TABLE 2.3

Doing Business in Indian Cities: Where is it Easiest?

Rank	*City*
1	Ludhiana, Punjab.
2	Hyderabad, Andhra Pradesh.
3	Bhubaneshwar, Odisha.
4	Gurgaon, Haryana.
5	Ahmedabad, Gujarat.
6	New Delhi, Delhi.
7	Jaipur, Rajasthan
8	Guwahati, Assam.
9	Ranchi, Jharkhand.
10	Mumbai (formerly called Bombay), Maharashtra.
11	Indore, Madhya Pradesh.
12	NOIDA, Uttar Pradesh.
13	Bengaluru (formerly called Bangalore), Karnataka
14	Patna, Bihar.
15	Chennai (formerly called Madras), Tamil Nadu.
16	Kochi, Kerala.
17	Kolkata (formerly called Calcutta), West Bengal.

Table 2.3 is an eye-opener. Gujarat and Tamil Nadu are widely cited to be the best states for business, yet their top cities rank at only 5th and 15th position respectively. Maharashtra is India's most industrialised state. Yet its capital Mumbai comes way down the list at 10th position. This suggests that in some of the top destinations, the political-bureaucratic system is often designed to create hurdles, requiring the payment of "speed money" for clearances. Some of the more advanced states can get away with this: they are confident that corporations simply have to invest there. This has left some scope for the less popular investment destinations to offer a better business climate. Punjab is at the forefront of this.

Starting a business

The 2009 report looks at several different aspects of doing business. A key issue is the ease of starting a business. The report measures this by estimating the time and cost of all starting steps including permits, inscriptions, notifications and inspections. New Zealand is champion in this respect—starting a business requires only 1 procedure and takes only 1 day. Eastern Europe and Northern Africa are not far behind. Georgia has 3 procedures that take just 3 days and Egypt manages in 7 days. But in Indian cities, the average number of procedures is 12. These take on average 34 days and cost 47 per cent of per capita income (against 0.4% in New Zealand, 6% in South Africa and 8% in China). In Ludhiana, starting a business takes 33 days, somewhat more than in Mumbai (30 days) but far better than Kochi (41 days) or Bengaluru (40 days). Surprisingly, China's average is worse than even India's (40 days against 34 days), despite its reputation for getting things done in fast autocratic fashion (see Figure 2.1).

FIGURE 2.1

Time and Cost to Start a Business in India and Selected Economies

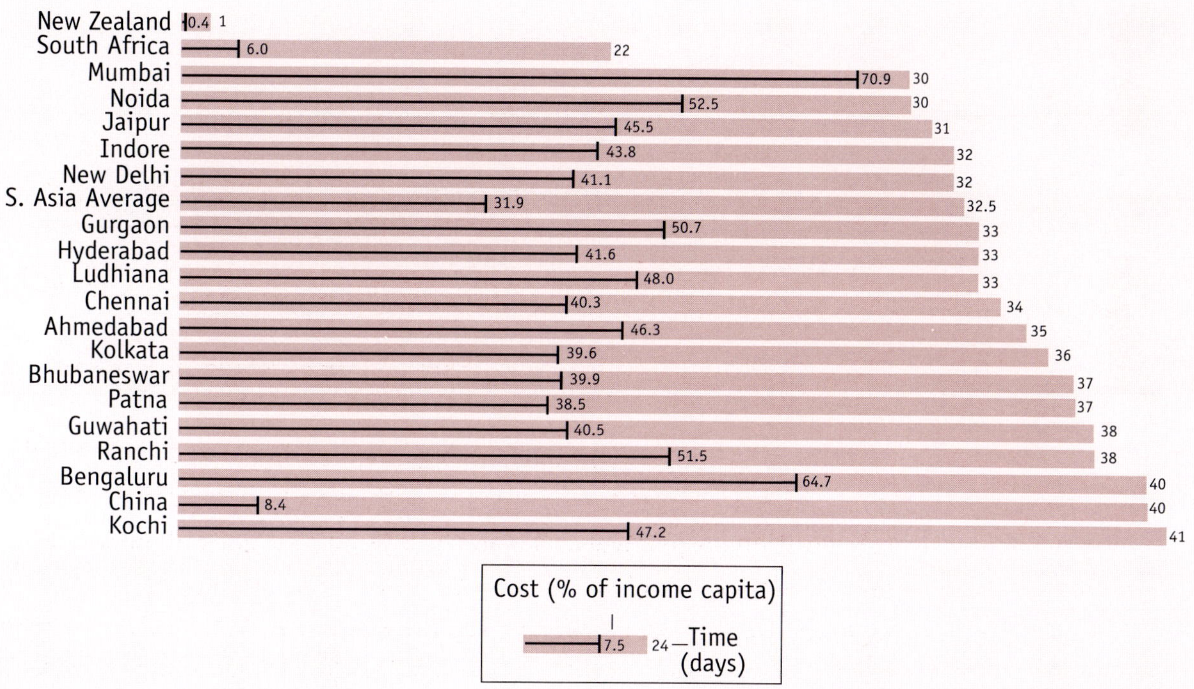

Source: *Doing Business* database.

Getting construction permits

This is a major hurdle in all Indian cities. The average for the 17 cities was 20 different procedures taking 158 days and costing 772 per cent of per capita income. However, this is better than in neighbouring South Asian countries, where getting a construction permit takes 246 days and costs 2,341 per cent of per capita income.

Ludhiana, Punjab, comes 7th of the 17 cities. It has 17 procedures taking 143 days. Bengaluru fares far better with 15 procedures taking 97 days. But Ludhiana is far better than Kolkata and Mumbai, which have 27 and 37 procedures respectively and take 258 and 200 days respectively. The total cost as a proportion of per capita income is 623 per cent in Ludhiana, compared with 2,718 per cent in Mumbai (see Figure 2.2).

FIGURE 2.2

Building Permit Approvals and Utility Connections: The Biggest Bottlenecks

Source: *Doing Business* database.

Registering property

This is another area marked by cumbersome procedures, delays and corruption. In Saudi Arabia, property can be registered in just 2 days at zero cost. Brazil and China also have zero cost of registration, through they take 29 days and 42 days respectively. But in India, the average registration time in the 17 cities is 55 days, and the cost is a whopping 10.6 per cent of the property value. These costs arise out of high stamp duties, registration costs and lawyers' fees (see Figure 2.3).

FIGURE 2.3

Time and Cost to Register Property in India and Selected Economies

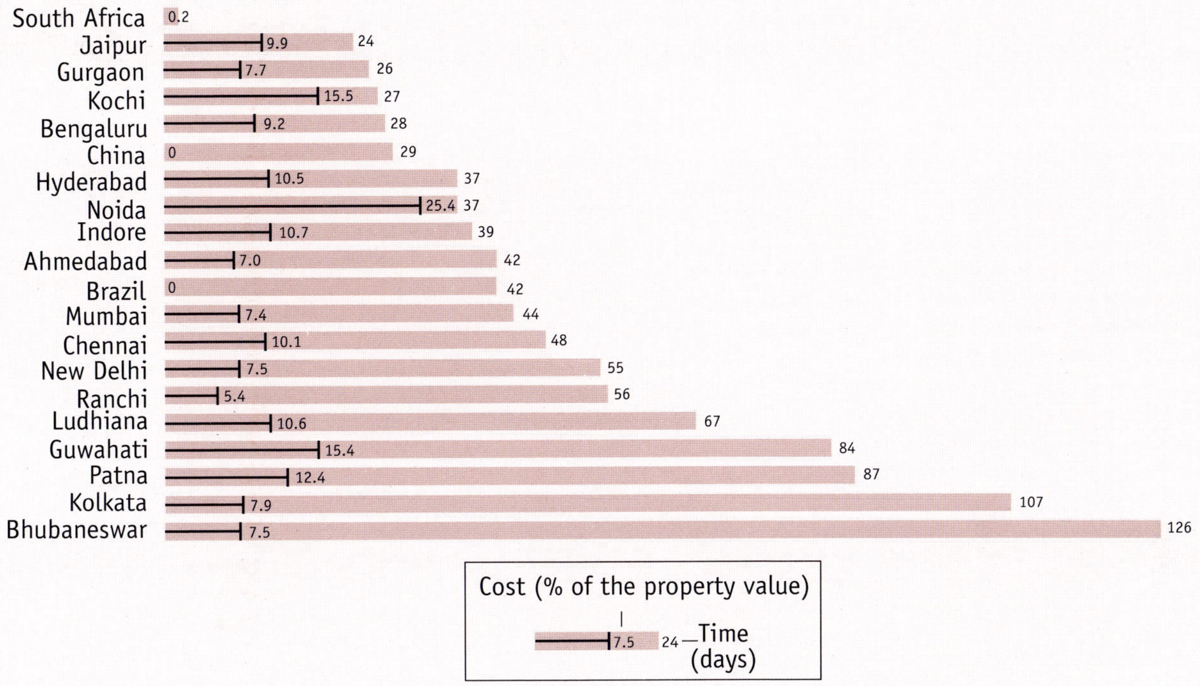

Source: *Doing Business* database.

Ludhiana, Punjab, is a laggard in this respect, coming 11th of 17 cities. The time taken in Ludhiana is 67 days. This is far behind Jaipur (24 days) but far ahead of Bhubaneshwar (126 days).

Paying taxes

Businesses pay a wide range of taxes at the central, state and local levels. There are taxes on production of goods and services, on the sale of goods and services, on transportation, on income. There are vehicle taxes, profession taxes, municipal taxes, environmental imposts and so on. *Doing Business in India 2009* also includes government-mandated contributions to employee provident funds and insurance funds. However, the calculation excludes value added taxes because these do not affect accounting profits.

In Hong Kong, a business spends on average 80 hours in 4 payments per year, adding up to 24.2 per cent of profits. But India ranks 169th of 183 countries in this respect. The average Indian business spends a whopping 278 hours on 65 different payments per year, adding up to 68.4 per cent of company profits. India's South Asian neighbours have only 37 payments per year aggregating 44.4 per cent of profits but this can take more time—336 hours per year.

Tax payments are a major irritant in Ludhiana too but the silver lining is that it is the best of the 17 Indian cities (see Table 2.4).

TABLE 2.4

Where it's Easiest to Pay Taxes in 17 Indian Cities

Rank	City
1	Ludhiana, Punjab.
2	Jaipur, Rajasthan.
3	NOIDA, Uttar Pradesh.
4	Mumbai, Maharashtra, and Ranchi, Jharkhand.
6	Guwahati, Assam.
7	Gurgaon, Haryana.
8	New Delhi, Delhi.
9	Bhubaneshwar, Odisha.
10	Indore, Madhya Pradesh.
11	Ahmedabad, Gujarat.
12	Bengaluru, Karnataka.
13	Hyderabad, Andhra Pradesh.
14	Kochi, Kerala.
15	Patna, Bihar.
16	Kolkata, West Bengal.
17	Chennai, Tamil Nadu.

Ludhiana is joint number one with Bengaluru, Mumbai and NOIDA in the number of tax payments per year—59. A major industrial centre like Ahmedabad requires 75 payments and Hyderabad 78.

Trading across borders

Merchandise exports are around 15 per cent of GDP in India. Imports are almost 20 per cent of GDP. Ease of export and import is an important business consideration. Some cities are far inland, so businesses in such cities have to import and export goods through a distant port in another state. So, the ease of trade depends on central government regulations as well as those in the port states and inland states.

In this respect, Ludhiana comes only 12th of 17 cities. This reflects in part its land-locked position: being far inland handicaps it relative to port cities. Other cities close to Ludhiana rank lower—Jaipur and New Delhi rank joint 14th, NOIDA (on the periphery of Delhi) comes 16th, and Gurgaon (also on Delhi's periphery) comes 17th. So, Punjab can claim that it beats the nearby competition (see Table 2.5).

TABLE 2.5

Where it's Easiest to Import and Export

Rank	*City*
1	Bhubaneshwar, Odisha.
2	Chennai, Tamil Nadu.
3	Ahmedabad, Gujarat and Mumbai, Maharashtra.
5	Kochi, Kerala.
6	Kolkata, West Bengal
7	Guwahati, Assam.
8	Ranchi, Jharkhand.
9	Bengaluru, Karnataka.
10	Patna, Bihar.
11	Indore, Madhya Pradesh.
12	Ludhiana, Punjab.
13	Hyderabad, Andhra Pradesh.
14	Jaipur, Rajasthan, and New Delhi, Delhi.
16	NOIDA, Uttar Pradesh.
17	Gurgaon, Haryana.

The time taken to export a container of goods from Ludhiana is 21 days, against 22 in Jaipur, and 25 days in Gurgaon, New Delhi and NOIDA. Ahmedabad comes on top with 17 days.

The time taken to import a container of goods is 25 days for Ludhiana, somewhat better than 27 for NOIDA and 28 days for Gurgaon and New Delhi. Bhubaneshwar comes on top with 16 days, while Ranchi comes last with 36 days.

The cost of importing and exporting a container is an important determinant of ease of business. Of all the cities in our list, Ludhiana is the furthest from a port. It comes 16th of the 17 cities with an average export cost of $1,105 per container, and 13th in cost of import at $1,154. Kochi, Kerala and Jaipur, Rajasthan, are the best and worst respectively for both import and export cost. The cost of exporting a container is just $432 in Kochi and $541 in Chennai, but as high as $945 in another port city, Mumbai (see Figure 2.4).

FIGURE 2.4

Cost to Export and Import in India

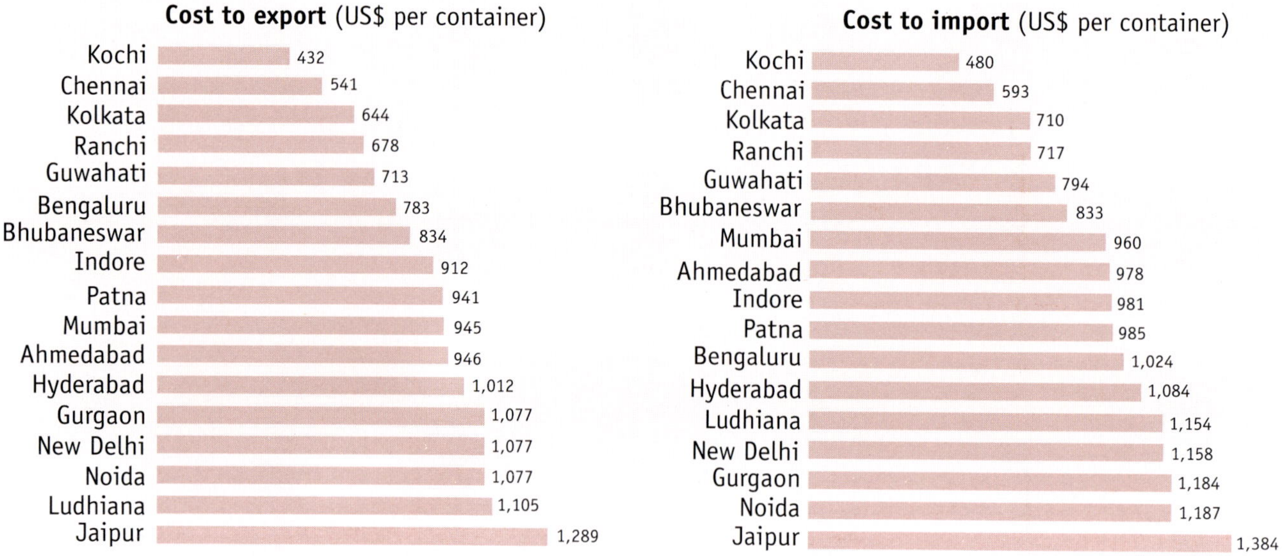

Source: *Doing Business* database.

Enforcing contracts

Strong enforcement is critical for business. But enforcement is terrible in India. The courts are so slow that most corporations try to settle disputes outside the courts. India is estimated to have barely 10.5 judges per million people, against the global norm of 50. The US has 107 judges per million population, and Canada has 75. Indian judges have to handle almost 4,000 cases each and the backlog of cases is overt one million.

It has barely one policeman per hundred thousand population, half the global norm. Besides, the police are deployed overwhelmingly in security for VIPs and maintenance of public order (India is a land of a thousand demonstrations and riots). Very limited police resources are left for crime detection, or for pursuing cases in courts.

TABLE 2.6

Where Enforcing Contract is Easiest

Rank	*City*
1	Hyderabad, Andhra Pradesh.
2	Guwahati, Assam.
3	Patna, Bihar.
4	Ludhiana, Punjab.
5	Bhubaneshwar, Odisha.
6	Kochi, Kerala.
7	Japiur, Rajasthan, NOIDA, Uttar Pradesh and Chennai, Tamil Nadu.
10	Indore, Madhya Pradesh.
11	Ranchi, Jharkhand.
12	New Delhi, Delhi.
13	Kolkata, West Bengal.
14	Gurgaon, Haryana.
15	Bengaluru, Karnataka
16	Ahmedabad, Gujarat.
17	Mumbai, Maharashtra.

Remarkable, most of India's biggest business centres come at the bottom of this list—Mumbai, Ahmedabad, Bengaluru, Gurgaon and New Delhi. Contract enforcement is, paradoxically, much better in what are often regarded as backward, badly administered states, such as Assam, Bihar and Odisha. Possibly the sheer volume of cases in the advanced, industrialised states overwhelms the judicial process and slows it to a crawl (see Table 2.6).

Ludhiana, Punjab, comes fourth in the list. That sounds good, but in absolute terms it is pretty dreadful. Judgment plus enforcement takes on average almost two and a half years. The fastest in India is Guwahati at 600 days. Mumbai is at the very bottom, at 1,420 days—almost four years (see Figure 2.5).

The cost of enforcing contracts depends on attorney and court fees. Here again the most advanced industrialised states are the worst, while relatively backward states have relatively low costs. Ludhiana comes fourth in this respect, with costs of 20 per cent of a commercial contract. Patna is the cheapest at 16 per cent. Mumbai is the most expensive at 39.5 per cent.

FIGURE 2.5

Lenghty Delays in the Judgement Phase across India

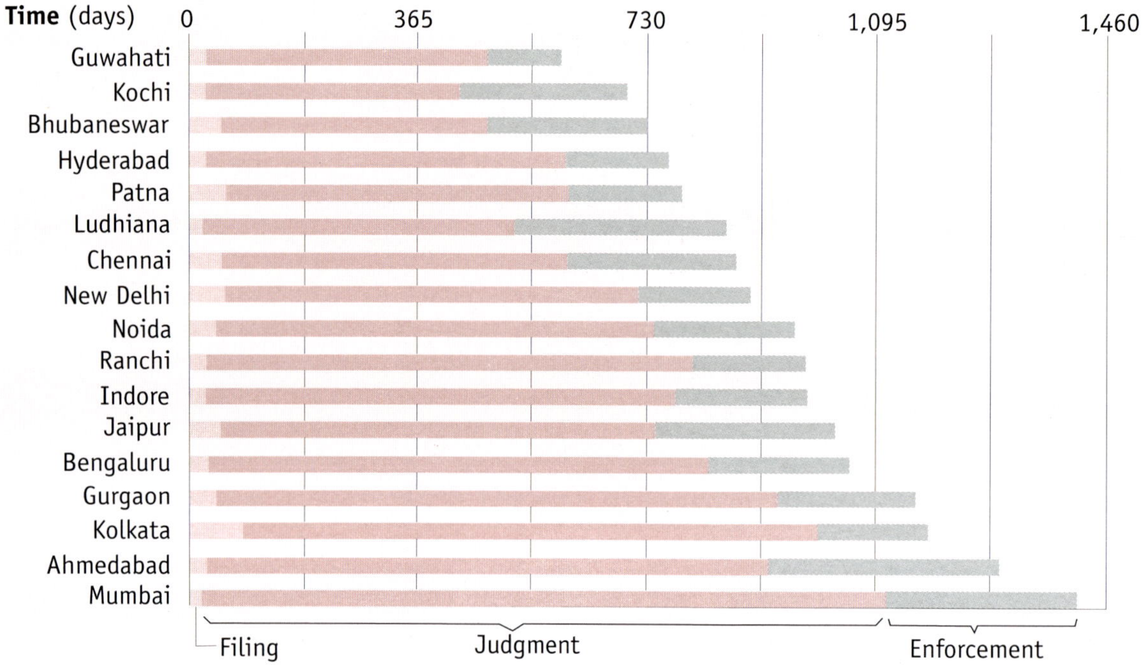

Source: *Doing Business* database.

Ease of closing a business

Capitalism is fundamentally a process of creative destruction. In India, closing a business is so slow and expensive that the normal churning of capitalism is severely hampered. Across the 17 cities, the insolvency process averages 7.9 years and costs 8.6 per cent of the estate's value. The actual amount recovered at the end of the process is a pathetic 13.7 cents in the dollar. In OECD countries the insolvency process takes just 1.7 years, and the recovery rate is five times higher at 68.6 cents in the dollar.

TABLE 2.7

Where it's Easiest to Close a Business.

Rank	*City*
1	Hyderabad, Andhra Pradesh.
2	Ludhiana, Punjab.
3	Mumbai. Maharashtra.
4	Ahmedabad, Gujarat.
5	Bhubaneshwar, Odisha.
6	Gurgaon, Haryana and New Delhi, Delhi.
8	Bengaluru, Karnataka.
9	Indore, Madhya Pradesh.
10	Chennai, Tamil Nadu and Kochi, Kerala.
12	Guwahati, Assam.
13	Ranchi, Jharkhand.
14	Jaipur, Rajasthan.
15	Patna, Bihar.
16	NOIDA, Uttar Pradesh.
17	Kolkata, West Bengal.

In this respect, Ludhiana comes second in the list of 17 cities. However, no state wants to boast about ease of closure—this is politically not palatable. So Punjab cannot trumpet this as a good reason for businesses to invest there (see Table 2.7).

The overall verdict on Ludhiana is favourable. Despite many shortcomings, Ludhiana's high rank shows that Punjab has made a commendable effort to create a good business climate at the city level. *Caveat*: being the best of Indian cities does not at all mean being good by international standards. India ranks so low on ease of doing business—just 134th of 183 countries—that every Indian city has a long way to go (see Table 2.8).

TABLE 2.8

Ludhina, Punjab: Doing Business

Ease of doing business (rank)	1				
Starting business (rank)	7	**Paying taxes (rank)**	1	**Enforcing contracts (rank)**	4
Procedures (number)	12	Payments (number per year)	59	Procedures (number)	46
Time (days)	33	Time (hours per year)	255	Time (days)	862
Cost (% of income per capita)	48	Total tax rate (% of profit)	67.6	Cost (% of claim)	20
Minimum capital (% of income per capita)	0				
		Trading across borders (rank)	12	**Closing business (rank)**	2
Dealing with construction permits (rank)	7	Documents to export (number)	8	Time (years)	7.3
Procedures (number)	17	Time to export (days)	21	Cost (% of estate)	7
Time (days)	143	Cost to export (US $ per container)	1,105	Recovery rate (cents on the dollar)	15.3
Cost (% of income per capita)	622.9	Documents to import (number)	9		
		Time to import (days)	25		
Registering property (rank)	11	Cost to import (US $ per container)	1,154		
Procedures (number)	4				
Time (days)	67				
Cost (% of the property value)	10.6				

Conclusion, and the Way Forward

Once regarded as India's most dynamic and progressive state, Punjab has slipped relative to other states. It remains reasonably prosperous and fast growing but its growth has dipped below the national average. To regain its place in the sun, its politicians need to abandon old myths about why Punjab is in trouble and face up to some ugly realities. The state needs to tackle its chronic fiscal deficit, something that holds back investment in education, health and infrastructure, and focuses public spending on various unproductive subsidies, the most fiscally crippling of which is free power for farmers. It needs to end perverse incentives that encourage land speculation and push up land prices so high as to make industrial investment uneconomic. It needs to end chronic power shortages and rehabilitate the state's deteriorating transmission system and this cannot be done without charging farmers for power. Agricultural marketing is riddled with controls and needs to be freed from the grip of a trading class with huge political clout.

The positive news is that Punjab has managed to attract private investment in power, so electricity shortages should lessen in coming years. It has also shifted from old public sector monopolies to PPP in health, education and infrastructure, and these promise to improve efficiency and outcomes as well as accelerate investment. Its Right to Service Act is a promising first step in improving administrative efficiency and justice for citizens. Punjab has recently allowed long-term farm leases and this could attract big investments and raise productivity in agriculture. It has a good business climate by Indian standards—Ludhiana is ranked the most business-friendly of the country's top 17 cities. The best recent news is that trade between India and Pakistan looks like getting normalised after decades of bitter hostility and confrontation. Punjab looks like becoming the gateway of Indian trade with Pakistan and that will give its economy a big boost. It needs to build on this.

End notes

1. Kang, Bhavdeep (2012). "Green Revocation", *India Today*. August 9.
2. *Budget 2011-12*. Punjab Government April 2011.
3. Central Statistical Organisation Databook, November 1st 2011.
4. Aiyar, Swaminathan S. Anklesaria (2012). "Akalis have shown that a bankrupt state can win elections, but is this sustainable? Probably not", *The Economic Times*, March 14.

5. *Doing Business in India 2009*. World Bank, June 30, 2009

6. Conversations in March 2012 of the author with Prof Gurmail Singh, Punjab University; Prof Surinder Shukla, Punjab University; Profs Such Singh Gill and Ranjit Ghuman, CRRID, Chandigarh; S.S. Johl, former head of Punjab Agricultural University.

7. Verma, Nidhi (2012). "India holds talks over fuel exports to Pakistan", *Reuters*. April 28.

8. Conversation of author with Prof Gurmail Singh of Punjab University, Chandigarh, in March 2012.

9. Punjab Budget speech. *http://punjabgovt.nic.in/departments/Budget/budget/budget.html.*

10. Conversation with V.S. Senthil of the Indian Administrative Service in March 2012.

11. See *World Development Indicators 2012*. World Bank. Link: *data.worldbank.org/data-catalog/world-development-indicators*.

12. Conversations with Profs. Gurmail Singh, Surinder Shukla, Sucha Singh Gill and S.S. Johl in March 2012.

13. P.S. Dhindsa, speech of Finance Minister, *Punjab Budget*, June 2012

14. Aiyar, Swaminathan S. Anklesaria (2012). "Akalis have shown that a bankrupt state can win elections, but is this sustainable? Probably not", *The Economic Times*, March 14.

15. Conversation with S.S. Johl, March 2012.

16. Conversation with Prof Gurmail Singh, Punjab University, March 2012.

17. Conversation with Prof Surinder Shukla, March 2012.

18. Coversation with Prof Gurmail Singh, March 2012.

19. Conversation wit Raj Chengappa, Editor, The Tribune, Chandigarh, Match 2012.

20. Rao, M Govinda (2012). *States' Fiscal Development and Implications for Regional Development*, National Institute of Public Finance and Policy, August.

21. Aiyar, Swaminathan S. Anklesaria (2012). "Akalis have shown that a bankrupt state can win elections, but is this sustainable? Probably not", *The Economic Times*, March 14.

22. Sen, Amiti (2012). "India seeks Pak nod for trade via land", *The Economic Times*, New Delhi, August 7.

23. Ahmed, Sadiq and Ejaz Ghani (eds.) (2007). *South Asia: Growth and Regional Integration*. World Bank.

24. Conversation with Pramod Kumar, former Chairman Punjab Governance Reforms Commission, in March 2012.

25. Gupta, Dipankar (2012). Comments at seminar on *Growth, Poverty and Human Development in Indian States: Selected Issues* in New Delhi, organised by Columbia University and National Institute of Public Finance and Policy on August 7.

26. Conversation with Pramod Kumar, former Chairman, Punjab Governance Reforms Commission, in March 2012.

27. Press release of the Confederation of Indian Industries. "CII urges states to replicate land reforms initiated by Punjab and Rajasthan", September 27, 2011.

28. *Doing Business in India*. World Bank. June 30, 2009.

3

How to Create Economic Freedom for Agriculture

Can Agriculture be Unshackled from Government Controls?

Ashok Gulati

On the face of it, Indian agriculture is country's largest private sector enterprise employing more than half the workforce and contributing about 14 per cent to overall GDP of the country. Given that it is in private sector, one would expect that this sector should enjoy full freedom to produce whatever it likes, market its produce the way it deems fit, both at home and abroad and buy its inputs from anyone it prefers. This expectation is particularly strong since the economic reforms of 1991 have freed many controls on industry. But the reality is that agriculture is still a sector that has the most stifling controls, especially on marketing its produce.

In this brief chapter, first we highlight the nature and degree of government interventions in three agricultural products and two basic inputs (land and water) as examples of the overall malaise. Then we try to see whether the government has been able to achieve its stated objectives through these controls. If so, we see at what cost, especially in terms of production and marketing efficiency and also in terms of overall growth of that sector. Finally, we present what could be the way forward to ensure faster and more inclusive growth in agriculture, more efficiency in production and marketing, and more sustainability in environmental and financial terms.

The author is Chairman of the Commission for Agricultural Costs and Prices, Government of India. Views expressed in this paper are purely personal and do not in any way reflect the view of the Commission, or Government of India.

Sugar: Controls and Consequences

Consider the following. An official in the Directorate of Sugar (Government of India) decides how much sugar each of the 550-plus sugar mills in the country can sell as "non-levy quota" in the free market each month. Sometimes this so-called "release mechanism" is used to control sugar sales every fortnight, or even every week. An overall "export quota" for sugar exports is decided in tranches by an Empowered Group of Ministers (a Cabinet sub-committee), over several meetings. Then another official decides how much of the government's annual "export quota" should be allotted to each sugar mill and how much they can export each month (whether or not they have the international competitiveness or motivation to export). Mills are also subject to a "levy-quota": each mill has to give the government a portion of its output at a below-market price fixed by the government, for distribution at subsidised rates to consumers served by the public distribution system (PDS). The levy quota has varied over time: it was once as high as 65 per cent but is currently 10 per cent. However, it can be raised any time the government feels the need to do so.

The government also decides whether the packing of sugar will be in jute bags or poly-propylene bags (this allows it to provide artificial respiration to a dying, uneconomic jute industry). The by-products of sugar are also controlled. Molasses generally cannot move from one state to another, unless permitted by the state government. Molasses cannot be sold freely: different industrial users (mainly liquor and chemicals) are allotted quotas of molasses by state governments. Whether sugar mills can produce ethanol from sugarcane or molasses has to be decided by the government (and permission has been refused for several mills in Bihar). The price of ethanol too is decided by the government. So too is the price of electricity generated from bagasse (crushed cane). Controls abound at not only the factory level but trade level too. How much sugar or molasses can be held by any wholesale trader or sugar factory at any particular time is decided periodically by some official.

Sugarcane is a starting point for many industries—liquor, ethanol, chemicals, electricity, fibre board. When the marketing and pricing of sugar as well as allied products is subject to government controls (which are sometimes light-years from market rationality), the potential of developing sugarcane is affected. The price of cane to be paid by sugar factories to farmers is announced by the Central government. This is supposed to be a fair and remunerative price (FRP) based on the recommendations of the Commission for Agricultural Costs and Prices (CACP). But then different states, most notably Uttar Pradesh, announce their own "State Advised Price" (SAP). This can be much higher than the fair price announced by the Central government and this often makes the FRP irrelevant. The state of Maharashtra has its own system of cane pricing, which also is much higher than the FRP announced by the Centre.

The impact of these controls on the growth and efficiency of cane production and the sugar industry is a matter for detailed research. But what is very clear is that despite industrial delicensing of this sector and opening it to foreign direct investment (FDI), it has failed to attract any. Investment has come primarily from the Indian private sector, and that too when packaged with large tax concessions (which can, however, be withdrawn arbitrarily). Sugar production in Maharashtra is done by cooperatives. Once viewed as a model, the Maharashtra regime is under severe strain and fragmenting. It cannot compete with the private sector which has scale economies. Maharashtra has a severe dearth of water, and so is not suitable for a water-guzzling crop like cane. Less than 3 per cent of the state's cropped area is under sugarcane but it uses more than 60 per cent of the irrigation water of the state. Ironically, sugar factories have gone sick in a state like Bihar which has ample water and so used to be the hub of sugarcane cultivation 100 years ago.

Sugar factories often complain of a "political overdose" in the pricing of cane at the state level (through SAPs). This is especially true during election years, when the ruling party woos farmers with sky-high cane prices. Quite often this makes factories unable to pay farmers in full and leads to large payment arrears. In April 2012, the cumulative payment arrears were estimated at ₹ 10,000 crores (around $200 million). Payments disputes drag on in the courts for years.

The ratio of Central government cane prices to market price for sugar was just 46 per cent in the period 2002-03 to 2006-07, way below the international norm of 70 per cent. So if farmers had always been paid the low price fixed by the central government, India's sugar industry would have been much smaller. The SAPs have been closer to international prices. For example, in the state of Uttar Pradesh, the cane-to-sugar price ratio was 69.4 in 2004-05 to 2008-09. In Maharashtra, this percentage was even higher at 74.3 per cent for the same period (because the sugar yield per tonne of cane is much higher in Maharashtra than in Uttar Pradesh). All such pricing is arbitrary and unrelated to market realities. This greatly hampers investment in cane and sugar by farmers and mills.

Rice: Controls and Consequences

Consider the case of India's biggest staple crop, rice. India is the world's second largest producer of rice (after China), growing 103 million tonnes (m.t.) of rice from 44 million hectares in 2011-12. There are many controls. The central government banned exports of rice in the wake of skyrocketing global prices in 2007-08. Some states like Andhra Pradesh have banned the movement of rice out of the state. This has happened even though four of the last five years have witnessed normal rainfall in India, resulting in rice production rising from 96 million tonnes in 2007-08 to 103 million tonnes in 2011-12. High production plus export restrictions have led to accumulation of rice and wheat stocks with the government. These rose from 24 m.t. on July 1st, 2007 to an estimated 75 m.t. by the end of June 2012. The covered capacity to store grain in the country is less than 50 million tonnes, so the rest of the grain is being stacked in the open and covered with plastic sheets, exposing it to potential damage during the rainy season.

In the 2010-11 post-monsoon marketing season, the national export ban on rice, coupled with inter-state restrictions in Andhra Pradesh, created a crisis. The market price of paddy in Andhra Pradesh crashed below the government's own minimum support price (MSP). Angry farmers swore to respond with a "crop holiday". In consequence, the rice area in Andhra Pradesh came down from 4.8 million hectares in 2010-11 to 4 million hectares in 2011-12.

The Commisson on Agricultiural Prices and Costs (CACP) in its 2011-12 Policy Report urged the government to restart exports of rice and wheat. This prompted the government to open up exports of rice in September 2011. It is expected that in 2011-12, India will export more than 6.5 m.t. of rice. This saved Andhra Pradesh farmers from another "price crash"—the maximum exports of rice took place from this state. However, farmers in Assam, Bihar, Jharkhand, Odisha, eastern Uttar Pradesh and West Bengal suffered from market prices way below the government's promised minimum. Clearly, export controls inflict an implicit tax on paddy farmers, who suffer depressed prices.

Paddy has to be sent to mills for rice extraction. In each major rice-growing state, rice mills are obliged to give a certain percentage of rice milled to the government at a fixed price—this is called "levy rice". This provides the government with rice for its subsidised public distribution system (PDS). The levy on rice ranges from 75 per cent of milled common rice in Punjab, Haryana, Andhra Pradesh to 50 per cent in Uttar Pradesh and West Bengal.

State governments decide how much rice wholesale traders can hold at any time. The rice market is also burdened with some other controls. Punjab, for example, imposes local taxes totaling 14.5 per cent of paddy price. In Andhra Pradesh local levies total 12.5 per cent, and in Haryana 11.5 per cent. These amount to taxes on consumers in rice-deficit states. High levies keep much of the private trade away, and this has led to a virtual state take-over of trade in paddy/rice in these states. Chhattisgarh is the latest state entering this category.

A state like Kerala gives paddy farmers an extra bonus of ₹ 500 ($10) per quintal over and above the central government's MSP. Kerala also provides a subsidy of ₹ 10,000 ($200)/hectare to grow paddy, creating a Japan-like island of high cost paddy cultivation within India. This plethora of government interventions seriously distorts the rice market and leads to irrational incentives and disincentives. The problem gets compounded when some states sell rice to the poor at just ₹ 1 per kilogram (as in Andhra Pradesh, Tamil Nadu and Kerala). This can be sold right back to the governments at a huge profit at the next harvest, at the MSP. India needs a unified national market, with rice flowing seamlessly across state borders. Instead we have a highly fragmented rice market, leading to large inefficiencies in production, procurement, stocking and distribution.

Heavy national reliance on Punjab for procuring rice for the PDS has led to serious environmental problems. The state's ground water table has fallen calamitously. The majority of its districts have been declared in danger or in crisis, with water withdrawals vastly exceeding annual recharge by rain. On the other hand Bihar, eastern Uttar Pradesh and West Bengal have ample water and are ideal for paddy cultivation. But the government has not organised procurement from these states at the MSP, as it has in Punjab. So, farmers in the eastern states with ample water end up getting paddy prices 20 to 30 per cent below what Punjab farmers get. This highlights huge inefficiencies in the rice system. Paddy is grown mostly where it should not be (Punjab) and much less where it should be (the eastern states).

Fruits and Vegetables (F&V): Controls and Consequences

Next, consider the case of F&V. These today account for almost one-fifth of the value of total agricultural output and demand for them is growing much faster than for cereals. In most states, F&V have to be sold through regulated markets (*mandis*). These have been set up under the APMC (Agricultural Produce Marketing Committe) Act. The biggest APMC markets for F&V are at Azadpur in Delhi and Vashi in Mumbai. The

APMC commission agents who conduct auctions of produce in Azadpur are officially entitled to charge 6 per cent commission on the value of transaction but field visits by researchers suggest that they charge up to 10 per cent with impunity. In Vashi, the official commission rate is 8 per cent but unofficially field reports suggest that it goes up to 14-15 per cent. An auction takes just five to ten minutes, so the commission agents are making easy monopoly profits without taking any risk of production or marketing.

Very little major investment has been made by state governments in building supply lines with good infrastructure. Cold chains—cold storages and refrigerated vans and trains—are needed for perishable products but are not available.

Produce should be sourced directly from farmers, not routed through commission agents at *mandis*, as mandated by the APMC Act. Unfortunately, organised retail remains at a nascent stage in India and FDI (foreign direct investment) in multibrand retail has not been permitted, despite discussions for almost a decade. This makes India's supply chains expensive with several layers of middlemen, gives lower prices to producers, yet charges high prices to consumers. This is neither efficient nor equitable. The system needs to be changed drastically. But this is resisted by the traders and middlemen, who are politically powerful.

Land and Water: Primary Inputs into Agriculture

The last example we would like to give constitutes the very base of agriculture, namely land and water. In case of land markets, most states do not permit tenancy at all. In those that permit it, the tenancy law is strongly tilted to protect tenant's rights and tenure, making it risky for owners to rent their land. Eviction is very difficult. According to large official surveys of the National Sample Survey Organisation (NSSO), tenancy exists on only 7 per cent of agricultural land. However, unofficial micro-surveys indicate that almost 30 per cent of land is leased in or leased out, mostly informally. Problem: the informal tenants find it difficult to get institutional credit as they have no land records to prove they are farmers. They are obliged to go to money lenders at 3 to 6 times bank rates of interest. This leads to high debt burdens and sometimes to suicides. In some states like Madhya Pradesh, Chhattisgarh and Bihar, tenant-farmers find it hard to sell their produce to government agencies, which also ask for land records. So, they are forced to sell to millers and traders, sometimes at a distress price. Investments in land suffer, as neither the landowner nor the tenant find it worthwhile to put much capital into the land, given uncertainties of sales.

Canal water and electricity for irrigation are provided to farmers by the government, mostly at very low rates or completely free. Since demand for such subsidised inputs greatly exceeds the supply, the quantity farmers get has to be rationed by government agencies. They limited the number of connections, limit hours of electricity supplied and days on which canal water is released into canals. Where states charge for electricity, it is generally a flat monthly rate per horse-power, with no electricity meters. The marginal cost of pumping becomes zero. This induces farmers to grow inappropriate water-intensive and electricity-intensive crops such as paddy and sugarcane even in low-rainfall areas. For example, paddy in Punjab and Haryana requires roughly 225 centimeters (cms.) of irrigation water per crop. But the annual rainfall is only 60 cms. So, farmers have to pump huge amounts of ground water for thirsty paddy, depleting the water table at an alarming rate (33 cms. per year, according to NASA satellites during 2002-2008). Similarly, sugarcane in Maharashtra demands large quantities of water and hogs the very limited water available from irrigation canals. These are more than environmental disasters in the making: they also ruin the finances of State Electricity Boards (SEBs) and Irrigation Departments.

The underpricing of water and power has led to another perverse outcome. Because competitors abroad have to pay for water and power, Indian producers of water/power guzzling crops appear to have greater export competitiveness. In 2011-12, India has exported more than 6.5 million tonnes of rice and more than 3 million tonnes of sugar. To produce a kilogram of rice, one requires 3,000-5,000 litres of water and the same is true of sugar. By exporting these large quantities of rice and sugar, we are basically exporting huge amounts of water. This is outrageous in a country where water is scarce and state governments fight each other bitterly over sharing river waters. Agricultural exports may look good but we need to ask whether our policies and controls have helped to develop cropping patterns and exports in line with India's natural endowments. The answer is "no". In which case, such exports are not sustainable.

The Way Forward: Dismantle the Controls and Free Agriculture

Where do we go from here? What changes in policy agenda will promote efficiency and growth that is widespread and inclusive? How should we promote sustainability, both financially and environmentally?

First, we must free up agriculture from domestic controls to the extent feasible. In case of sugar and sugarcane, controls such as release mechanisms, levy quotas, stocking limits, cane area reservation, minimum distance between sugar mills and several other minor controls all need to be removed. This will create greater competition, efficiency and growth. Similarly, we must abolish controls such as government levies on rice and paddy, movement restrictions across states, and stocking limits with traders and millers.

Second, physical bans on export/import of agricultural products must end. As a first step, they can be replaced by variable tariffs (import or export duties).

Third, crops like F&V need to be freed from marketing controls ordained by obsolete APMC laws. Indeed, the APMC Act needs to be changed to encourage direct sourcing by retailers from farmers' groups, to compress supply chains by removing unnecessary middlemen, and to invest in back-end infrastructure. For this, organised retailers, both domestic and foreign, need to be encouraged and incentivised.

Fourth, land lease markets needs to be officially freed. Tenancy, including long-term tenancy, should be encouraged in a transparent manner. This will induce agglomeration of small uneconomic holdings into larger economic ones. The pricing of water and power needs to be rationalized. Institutional reforms can help cut costs of generation and distribution of power and water by public utilities.

Such market reforms can go a long way to promote efficiency, growth and sustainability in Indian agriculture. It will improve inclusiveness too, by inducing growth faster than 4 per cent per year in a sector that employs half of all Indians, mostly poor.

4

India's Segmented Labour Markets, Inter-State Differences, and the Scope for Labour Reforms

Bibek Debroy

The Indian labour market is segmented. It has a labour aristocracy of unionised workers who are highly paid and highly protected, along with an overwhelming mass of unorganised workers, many of whom are unable in practice to exercise even legal rights. The high protection given to organised workers creates labour rigidities that discourage employment and encourage capital-intensive modes of production. It discourages Chinese-scale investment in labour-intensive industries (like garments and footwear) where high labour flexibility may be required because of fluctuating demand from overseas markets in different seasons. This is one reason why barely one-tenth of all workers are in the formal or organised sector: companies are reluctant to add to their formal labour rolls. Thus the protected status of the labour aristocracy comes at the expense of the the nine-tenths of workers in the unorganised sector, who are unable to get formal sector jobs.

Many analyses of labour laws focus just on labour rigidities and flexibility in hiring and retrenchment. But we need to consider several other issues too relating to labour. One such issue is the existence of a host of obsolete rules and regulations (such as the need to maintain manual labour rolls: modern computerised records are not allowed in some states!). Another major problem is the "inspector raj"—the problem all enterprises face (but small ones most of all) in dealing with an army of corrupt inspectors. Yet others relate to limiting hours of operation for shops, or limiting hours for female employment.

In contrast with developed economies, and also in contrast with several developing economies, a large chunk of Indian employment occurs in the rural sector. Outside agriculture, informality can be defined in one of three different ways. First, there is a definition in terms of exemptions from paying indirect taxes. Second, there is a definition in terms of small-scale industry (SSI), which again is defined in terms of threshold levels of investment in plant and machinery. Third, there is a definition in terms of labour laws. That is, an enterprise is unorganised if it uses power and employs fewer than 10 people or does not use power and employs fewer than 20 people.[1] The last definition is the one that is used most often.

Some labour laws come under the jurisdiction of the central government, some in that of state governments and others in the Concurrent List (joint jurisdiction). Most labour laws are in the Concurrent List. At the state level, there can be two kinds of labour laws. First, where a basic Central statute already exists, there can be State-level amendments. Second, there can be *de novo* State laws in areas with no Central statutes. The Kerala Labour Laws (Simplification of Returns and Registers of Small Establishments) Act of 2002 is an instance. However, government labour regulations go well beyond the statutes. The statutes provide an enabling framework, within which administrative law is framed, consisting of rules, orders and regulations. The Factories Act, 1948, is statutory. But rules under the Factories Act, 1948, are executive in nature and are part of administrative law. The implication is clear: even with a given central government statute, labour regulations can vary widely across states.

State intervention is often equated with implementation of laws on industrial relations, but this is an oversimplification. Many State interventions, often obtuse and comic, are common in areas that have no direct bearing on industrial relations too, such as the number of urinals and spittoons! The Factories Act says that "the State Government may prescribe the number of latrines and urinals to be provided in any factory" and "may make rules prescribing the number of spittoons to be provided and their location in any factory." The State government may also make rules "requiring the provision therein of suitable places for keeping clothing not worn during working hours and for the drying of wet clothing."

Such intervention can become even more obtuse and unwarranted when it comes to rules issued under various Acts. They often prescribe practices that were common a century ago and ignore new realities brought by electricity or computers. For instance, some rules say that factories must be whitewashed (painted with white lime). Apparently plastic paint won't do. The Rules say earthen pots filled with water are required. Apparently mechanised water coolers won't suffice. Red-painted buckets filled with sand are required by the Rules. Fire extinguishers won't do. There must be crèches (day-care centres for liitle children) within the factory. Making transport arrangements for accessing crèches outside the factory won't be enough.

In many states, the Shops and Establishments Acts prescribe which day of the week must be observed as a weekly holiday. They impose restrictions on employing women outside what are perceived to be regular working-hours, a clause that adversely affects the efficient functioning of call-centres and discriminates against female employees. This is not the place to provide a comprehensive list but several instances can be cited to illustrate dysfunctional and unnecessary State intervention. Several inspectors can descend on a factory under assorted labour laws and a system of having a single inspector for all labour laws does not exist.

Nor is there any standardisation of documentation requirements or time periods for which records have to be kept. The laws and rules prescribe that manual records have to be maintained: electronic records are not acceptable. And so on. Such procedural problems characterise all three stages of an enterprise's operations—entry, functioning and exit. These impose high transaction costs that render Indian business uncompetitive. Part of the problem with administrative decisions is that they bestow a large degree of discretion on petty functionaries. These encourage corruption and rent-seeking. This is especially damaging for the small self-employed entrepreneur, who lacks scale economies to deal with a plethora of rules and inspectors.

It is difficult to quantify the extent of the "inspector raj", apart from occasional surveys undertaken by industry chambers. Not only are these perception-based, they tend to have very small samples. That apart, the extent of the inspector *raj* clearly varies from State to State. When business complains about the inspector *raj*, this is not necessarily in relation to labour laws. Several inspections are connected to taxation, or environment, or safety. The ICS (Investment Climate Survey) data do not suggest that inspections related to labour laws are particularly onerous. An average enterprise had 0.40 Central government inspections under the labour and social security category, and 1.76 state government inspections.[2] However, there was much variation across the States, ranging from 0.32 inspections in Delhi to 4.65 in Punjab. What matters is not just the number of inspections but the opportunity this gives inspectors to engage in corruption and rent-seeking. Thanks to their discretionary powers, they can threaten various kinds of harassment that could be fatal for the financial health of enterprises.

Some laws, statutory and administrative, and reform initiatives, are within the province of the Centre. But there is much variation across States. Some State governments (Andhra Pradesh, Gujarat, Karnataka, Madhya Pradesh, Maharashtra) wish to make labour laws flexible, in order to encourage investment and reduce differentials in the treatment or organised and unorganised labour. Flexibility has been sought particularly in special economic zones (SEZs) and other special enclaves. Some States have suggested there could be greater flexibility in hours of work, allowing women to work at night or in minimum wages. But these sorts of flexibility would require Central legislation, which is not on the anvil, and looks politically impossible right now. Since 1989, all governments in New Delhi have been coalitions, and these coalitions have typically lacked a majority in the Upper House of Parliament. This has made the passage of any legislation problematic. India is a unique country in that virtually all major political parties have a trade union wing. This means political parties are reluctant to legislate on labour flexibility, since this would antagonise their own trade union wings.

States such as Uttar Pradesh, Andhra Pradesh, Punjab, Gujarat, Karnataka, Orissa and Rajasthan have consciously tried to reduce the number of inspectors, and Gujarat, Punjab, Rajasthan and Maharashtra have introduced self-certification. In Uttar Pradesh, labour inspectors can carry out inspections only after consent has been obtained from someone of the rank of a Labour Commissioner or District Magistrate and advance information about the inspection has been provided. Rajasthan and Andhra Pradesh have exempted certain kinds of enterprises from the ambit of labour inspections. For instance, Andhra Pradesh has introduced self-certification for information technology (IT) services, IT-enabled services, bio-technology, export oriented units (EOUs), units in export processing zones (EPZs) and tourism-based enterprises. Rajasthan has done the same for IT, IT-enabled services and biotechnology. This is a second-best solution, since the inspector *raj* still flourishes for enterprises outside the enclaves. Uttar Pradesh's reforms focus on enclaves such as SEZs but its other aspects are more broad-based. Although there are wide State-level variations, the number of labour inspections has declined in some States after the liberalising reforms of 1991. Because it is politically difficult to tackle the inspector *raj* head on, politicians have attempted it only in selected enclaves.

We now turn to industrial relations. The three relevant statutes are the Contract Labour (Regulation and Abolition) Act, the Trade Unions Act and the Industrial Disputes Act (IDA). The third one is the most discussed. The Contract Labour (Regulation and Abolition) Act was never meant to prohibit contract labour. It provided central and state governments discretion in prohibiting contract labour in selected areas. States like Andhra Pradesh have introduced amendments relating to contract labour, separating core activities from non-core. But as regards the Trade Unions Act or the IDA, there is little States can do on their own.

Two academic studies have sought to directly compute the impact of IDA. The first, by Peter Fallon and Robert Lucas,[3] was published in 1991, and is dated. The second, by Timothy Besley and Roger Burgess in 2004,[4] is not only more recent but seeks to capture the impact of the IDA across States. It investigates whether the industrial relations climate in Indian states affected the pattern of manufacturing growth in the period 1958–1992 (well before the reform era of the last two decades). It codes all labour regulations as pro-labour (defined as making it difficult for managements to hire, discipline or retrench labour, or to close down losing units) or anti-labour. The study shows that states that amended the IDA (to the extent permitted by state-level jurisdiction) in a pro-worker direction experienced lowered output, employment, investment and productivity in registered or formal manufacturing. In contrast, output in unregistered or informal manufacturing increased. Regulation in a pro-worker direction was also associated with increases in urban poverty. Laws supposedly aimed at protecting labour actually ended up hurting the poor. The IDA did not help labour as a whole: it helped only the labour aristocracy.

Two caveats to the Besley and Burgess study are required. First, does it make sense to focus on IDA alone, to the exclusion of other labour laws? What about the impact of minimum wages legislation, the Shops and Establishments Act, inspections by inspectors or strikes and lockouts? Second, there is some subjectivity in the "anti-labour" (-1) or "pro-labour" (+1) coding given in Besley and Burgess. Two examples will illustrate the point. In 1982, Andhra Pradesh introduced an amendment that merged the powers of industrial tribunals and civil courts. This has been regarded as anti-labour but may very well have reduced transaction costs in resolving disputes. Alternatively, in 1974, Maharashtra introduced an amendment that reduced the qualifications of judges. This was coded as "0" or neutral but may well have increased the number of judges and reduced transaction costs.

As an alternative approach, a transaction cost-based labour law ecosystem index for India's states was worked out by TeamLease, a contract employment company. It found that Maharashtra is by far the best as measured by a good labour law and regulation index. Next come Karnataka and Punjab. Gujarat and Delhi follow, though they are not highly different from each other in terms of the index values. The worst States in this respect are West Bengal, J&K, Assam, Uttar Pradesh and Kerala.[5]

Clearly India needs to reduce rigidity in its labour laws, of which, Chapter V-B of IDA is one instance. This obliges any company with over 100 workers to get permission from the government before retrenching (dispensing with the services of) any employee, and this permission is rarely given. In Bangladesh, a worker can be retrenched after giving one month's notice to the worker. This helps explain how Bangladesh, once a negligible exporter of garments, has now overtaken India as a garment exporter.

Japan in the 1950s, the four East Asian tigers in the 1960s and 1970s, and then the south-east Asian tigers all became miracle economies by harnessing cheap labour for export-oriented industries. China is the latest and most successful example. But India has failed altogether to jump onto the labour-intensive bandwagon, and labour rigidity is the main reason. Employers dare not hire thousands of workers in massive factories (as in China) for fear of not being able to retrench them in the event of a sudden fall in export demand, or a change of seasons requiring a big change in the sort of garments to be produced. No exit translates into no entry for workers in large scale manufacturing. This perpetuates a situation where the organised sector accounts for barely one-tenth of workers.

While labour flexibility is important, gains can also be made by reforming other aspects of labour law, which are politically less controversial and so politically easier to implement. It is a mistake to equate labour reforms with changes in Chapter V-B of IDA (which limits retrenchment, layoffs and closure in factories with over 100 workers). The result has been a political refusal to contemplate even the less controversial laws, such as the abolition of obsolete clauses (like mandating manual registers instead of electronic), laws relating to the inspector *raj*, laws limiting shop hours, laws limiting female participation at night, and so on.

Even if it proves politically difficult to scrap Chapter V-B of IDA, it may be possible to segregate the layoff, retrenchment and closure provisions, providing some flexibility. The IDA was tightened over a period of time and its tightening offers insights into how it can be progressively relaxed too. Layoffs, retrenchment and closure are actually three separate concepts and reflect increasing degrees of severity. They must be unbundled. Layoffs and retrenchment are more acceptable to trade unions and political parties than closures.[6] Thus, it is easier to sell reforms that, to begin with, apply only to lay-offs and maybe to retrenchment but not closures. For lay-offs and retrenchment, if compensation is increased from 30 days pay per year worked to 45 days, political resistance may diminish. It might diminish even more if existing contracts are grandfathered and the new provisions apply only to new labour contracts.

Third, it should also be possible to amend the Constitution to move labour issues entirely to the State list. This will mean that any state wishing to have flexibile labour laws will be able to legislate accordingly and not have to wait for New Delhi's legislation on the matter. Economic reforms have increased competition between states to attract industry and this has induced some States to be more forthcoming in granting permissions to retrench labour under Chapter V-B, although others have not. A change in the Seventh Schedule would explicitly allow and expedite, without legal complications, some trends already in evidence in the states.

Almost the entire pro-reform literature focuses on raising the threshold for the application of Chapter V-B to cover enterprises with more than 1000 workers, ten times the current threshold of 100. This will discriminate against smaller enterprises but the only clear argument to this effect is found in the afore-mentioned report of the Planning Commission.[7] Raising the threshold to 1,000 workers will dilute the impact of a bad labour concept but will not do away with it. Even an increased threshold will have many of the same adverse consequences: it will favour capital-intensity and discriminate against labour-intensive factories that are appropriate at India's current level of development. Far better will be a return to the pre-1976 status of IDA, which made no reference to any threshold. This will imply a complete repeal of Chapter V-B. It may be politically impossible right now but is the direction in which we should move.

End Notes

1. Strictly speaking, this is a Factories Act definition.
2. See, Ahsan, A., C. Pages and T. Roy (2008). "Legislation, enforcement and adjudication in Indian labour markets: Origins, consequences and the way forward", in D. Mazumdar and S. Sarkar (eds.), *Globalization, Labor Markets and Inequality in India*. New York: Routledge.
3. Fallon, Peter R. and Robert E.B. Lucas (1991). "The impact of changes in job security regulations in India and Zimbabwe", *World Bank Economic Review* 5(3): 395-413, September. World Bank Group.
4. Besley, Timothy and Roger Burgess (2004). "Can labour regulation hinder ecohnomic performance? Evidfence from India", *Quarterly Journal of Economics*.
5. *India Labour Report 2006: A Ranking of Indian States by their Labour Ecosystem*. TeamLease Services.
6. Labour Bureau statistics show that between 1998 and 2005, between 2000 and 4000 workers were retrenched per year, with the numbers dropping sharply in 2006 and 2007, 2007 being the last year for which data are available. However, the number of units affected has continuously declined from

195 in 1998 to 23 in 2007. That is, fewer units are affected but the number of workers per affected unit has gone up. There has been a similar trend for lay-offs. Between 200 and 300 units were affected by lay-offs from 1998 to 2002. This dropped below 200 in 2003 and below 100 in 2006. Workers laid off have also declined from 45,243 in 1998 to 12,255 in 2005 and 6,992 in 2007.

7. An example is the *Report of Planning Commission's Task Force on Employment Opportunities, 2001, http://planningcommission.nic.in/aboutus/taskforce/tk_empopp.pdf*

Appendices

APPENDIX I

Variables and Methodology

Description of Variables used for Economic Freedom of the States of India 2011

Normalised Variables	*Variables*	*Units*	*Source*
Area 1: Size of government: Expenditures, taxes and enterprises			
GSDP/Revenue expenditure	GSDP at Current Prices	₹ Crore	CSO & estimates
	Revenue expenditure	₹ Crore	RBI, State Budgets
% of GSDP accounted for by public administration	% of GSDP accounted for by public administration	%	CSO
Total organised employment/ Government employment	Total employment in organised sector	in '000	Directorate General of Employment & Training, Ministry of Labour
	Total employment in government and quasi-government institutions	in '000	Directorate General of Employment & Training, Ministry of Labour
GSDP constant prices/ State taxes on income	GSDP (2004-05 prices)	₹ Lakh	CSO & estimates
	State revenues from income tax	₹ Lakh	State Finances, RBI
GSDP constant prices/ State taxes on property and capital transactions	GSDP (2004-05 prices)	₹ Lakh	CSO & estimates
	State revenues from taxes on property and capital transactions	₹ Lakh	State Finances, RBI
GSDP constant prices/ Taxes on commodities and services	GSDP (2004-05 prices)	₹ lakh	CSO & estimates
	State revenues from taxes on commodities and services	₹ Lakh	State Finances, RBI
Inverse of Stamp Duty Rate	Stamp Duty Rate	%	*www.indiaproperties.com*

contd...

...contd...

Normalised Variables	*Variables*	*Units*	*Source*
Area 2: Legal structure and security of property rights			
Total value of property recovered/Value of property reported stolen	Total value of property recovered	₹ Lakh	National Crime Records Bureau
	Total value of property reported stolen	₹ Lakh	
Total number of posts in judiciary/Vacant posts	Total judiciary posts sanctioned in district/ subordinate courts	Number	GoI
	Vacant posts of judicial officers in district/subordinate courts	Number	
Total cases/Economic offences	Total incidence of crimes under Indian Penal Code (IPC)	Number	National Crime Records Bureau
	Economic offences (criminal breach of trust, cheating and counterfeiting)	Number	
Cases completed by police/Total cases registered with police	Cases where investigation completed by police	Number	National Crime Records Bureau
	Total cases registered for investigation by police	Number	
Trials completed by courts/Total cases for trial by courts	Total number of trials completed by courts	Number	National Crime Records Bureau
	Total number of cases awaiting or undergoing trial by courts	Number	
Total Cases/Violent crimes	Total incidence of crimes under IPC	Number	National Crime Records Bureau
	Cases of murder, attempt to murder, culpable homicide not amounting to murder, rape, kidnapping and abduction, preparation and assembly for dacoity, robbery, riots, arson and dowry deaths	Number	

contd...

...contd...

Normalised Variables	*Variables*	*Units*	*Source*
Area 5: Regulation of labour, and business			
Yearly average of daily wages for harvesting (Males)/Minimum notified wages	Yearly average of daily wages for harvesting (Males)	₹	Labour Bureau, Ministry of Labour, Government of India
	Minimum notified wages	₹ per day	Wage Cell, Ministry of Labour, Government of India
Yearly average of daily wages for harvesting (Females)/Minimum notified wages	Yearly average of daily wages for harvesting (Females)	₹	Labour Bureau, Ministry of Labour, Governmenmt of India
	Minimum notified wages	₹ per day	Wage Cell, Ministry of Labour, Government of India
Total number of industrial workers/Man days lost in strikes and lockouts	Total number of industrial workers	Number	Annual Survey of Industries Data, Central Statistical Organisation
	Man days lost in strikes and lockouts	Number	Industrial Disputes in India, 2007-08, Ministry of Labour, Government of India
Minimum license fee for traders	Minimum license fee for traders (₹ Per Annum)	₹ per annum	Ministry of Agriculture, Government of India
Actual Industrial Entrepreneurs Memorandums (IEMs)/ Value of Proposed IEMs	Actual value of IEMs that were implemented	₹ Crore	Secretariat for Industrial Assistance, Government of India
	Total value of proposed IEMs	₹ Crore	Secretariat for Industrial Assistance, Government of India
Met peak demand/ Peak demand	Met peak demand for electricity	MW	Ministry of Power Government of India
	Peak demand for electricity	MW	
Total cases registered for corruption/Cases pending investigation	Total cases for investigation under prevention of corruption and related acts	Number	National Crime Records Bureau (NCRB)
	Cases pending investigation from previous year	Number	
Total cases registered for corruption/Persons arrested for corruption	Total cases for investigation under prevention of corruption and related acts	Number	NCRB
	Persons arrested under prevention of corruption and related acts	Number	

APPENDIX II

Detailed Methodology

The Economic Freedom Index has been calculated for 20 states of India. Ideally, all 35 states and union territories should have been included; however, data unavailability prevented this. As a result only those states and union territories are included, for which data were available for most of the variables that are used to construct the index. No imputations were made.

Further, many variables that would have found a suitable place in this index could not be included as data were not available for many states. Eventually 21 variables covering diverse aspects of economic freedom in different areas were utilised to arrive at the composite freedom index. There were a few variables for which data were not available for some of the 20 states. However, since the indicator was essential for the credibility of the index, such indicators were retained.

There are many different ways of constructing a composite index. One way of doing this is to assign subjective weights to different variables. However, in order to ensure objectivity, this ranking refrains from such an exercise. No subjective weights have been used and as a result each variable is considered to be equally important.

The following steps were followed in constructing the index:

- Identifying the appropriate variables: The variables in the freedom index were chosen to enable a comprehensive view of economic freedom could be obtained while working within the constraints of data availability.
- Normalising the variables: Indian states vary in geographical area, topography, social and economic milieu. Depending on the variable and what it aspires to measure, each variable has been appropriately 'normalised'.
- Comparability of data: Since data is collected at the state level, care has to be taken to ensure that the data are defined in the same way for different states and also that they are for the same time point. Further, since the ranking exercise implies that higher values reflect better performance, appropriate ratios have been developed. Often this implied taking an inverse of a particular indicator or subtracting a percentage from 100.
- Creating an index of each variable: While the composite index gives an overall view of freedom, it may be that while a state performs

extremely well in certain indicators, its performance may not be as satisfactory in others. An index of each variable or indicator is also constructed, so that a ranking of the states is available for a detailed understanding of the situation of freedom. Details of the construction of individual indices are presented below.

- Creating a composite index for each category: The simple arithmetic mean was used to calculate the category indices.
- Calculating a composite/overall index: This final step required all three category indices to be aggregated to arrive at a composite indicator of relative economic freedom for 20 states.

The last three steps in constructing the economic freedom index are now explained in detail.

Creating an index of each variable: An index is obtained for each of the 24 ratios as mentioned earlier. The following formula was used to obtain each of the 24 indices:

$$I_{ij} = \frac{S_{ij} - Min(S_{1j}, S_{2j}, \ldots, S_{20j})}{Max(S_{1j}, S_{2j}, \ldots s_{20j}) - Min(S_{1j}, S_{2j}, \ldots, S_{20j})}$$

Where Sij represents the value of ratio j for state i. The index is constructed for 20 states of India and therefore i ranges from 1 to 20. There are 21 ratios for which the indices have been constructed, j=1,2,... 24. Iij is the index value that is derived for state i over ratio j. The index value lies between 0 to 1 for each ratio. The state corresponding to index value 0 can be interpreted as having the lowest level of economic freedom and the state with index value of 1 can be said to have the highest level of economic freedom relative to other states.

Note that the maximum and minimum values are the same as those used for earlier years, this ensures that the index values are comparable over time.

Creating a composite index for each category: Arithmetic mean was used to calculate the category index as follows:

$$C_{ik} = \frac{\sum_{j}^{n} I_{ijk}}{n}$$

Where C_{ik} is the category index of the ith state for the kth category over n indices within the category.

Calculating a composite/overall index: Once all the indices for the 24 ratios were obtained, a composite index was obtained using all these indices. An arithmetic mean of all the indices helped to arrive at the additive index. The formula used to calculate the composite index is as follows:

$$M_i = \frac{\sum_{k=1}^{N} C_{ik}}{N}$$

Where M_i is the additive index value for the ith state over the N category indices of freedom. Here N is 3.

APPENDIX III

Mapping of Variables with Economic Freedom of the World

EFW Categorisation		*Variables at the State Level for India*
Area 1: Size of government: Expenditures, taxes and enterprises		
a) General government consumption spending as a percentage of total consumption	1.	Government revenue expenditure/Gross State Domestic Product (GSDP)
	2.	Administrative GSDP/Total GSDP
b) Transfers and subsidies as a percentage of GDP	3.	Subsidy on power for domestic consumers/ Population
c) Government enterprises and investment as a percentage of GDP	4.	Govt. employment/Total organised employment
	5.	Percentage of state level public sector enterprises (SLPEs) in which Disinvestment completed or initiated
d) Top marginal tax rate (and income threshold to which it applies)	6.	State taxes on income/GDP
	7.	State taxes on property and capital transactions/GDP
	8.	Taxes on commodities and services/GSDP
	9.	Stamp duty rate
i. Top marginal tax rate (excluding applicable payroll taxes)		Data not available: also many different types of state income taxes
ii. Top marginal tax rate (including applicable payroll taxes)		
Area 2: Legal structure and security of property rights	10.	Total values of property recovered/ Total Value of property reported stolen
	11.	Vacant posts in judiciary as a ratio of total posts sanctioned
a) Judicial independence: the judiciary is independent and not subject to interference by the government or parties in disputes		Not Applicable
b) Impartial court: a trusted legal framework exists for private businesses to challenge the legality of government actions or regulation		
c) Protection of intellectual property		
d) Military interference in the rule of law and the political process		
e) Integrity of the legal system	12.	Cases under economic offences/Total cases
	13.	Per cent cases where trials were completed by courts
	14.	Per cent cases where investigations were completed by police
	15.	Violent crimes
Area 3: Access to sound money		
a) Average annual growth rate of money supply in the last 5 years minus average annual growth of real GDP in the last 10 years		Not Applicable

contd...

...contd...

EFW Categorisation		*Variables at the state level for India*
b) Standard inflation variability in the last 5 years		Inflation rate calculated on basis of GDP deflator
c) Recent inflation rate		
d) Freedom to own foreign currency bank accounts domestically and abroad		Not Applicable
Area 5: Regulation of credit, labour, and business		
a) Credit market regulations		
i. Ownership of banks: percentage of deposits held in privately owned banks		Financial sector overseen by central government, no state level differences
ii Competition- domestic banks face competition from foreign banks		
iii Extension of credit: percentage of credit extended to private sector		
iv Avoidance of interest rate controls and regulations that leas to negative real interest rates		
v Interest rate controls: interest rate controls on bank deposits and/or loans are freely determined by the market		
b) Labour Market Regulations		
i. Impact of minimum wage- minimum wage set by law has little impact on wages because it is too low or not obeyed	16.	Average wage of unskilled workers/ Minimum wages
ii. Hiring and firing practices- hiring and firing practices of companies are determined by private contract	17.	Man-days lost in strikes and lockouts/ total number of industrial workers
iii. Share of labor force whose wages are set by centralized collective bargaining	18.	Unorganised labour force as a ratio of organised labour force
iv. Unemployment benefits: the unemployment benefits system preserves the incentive to work		Not Applicable
v Use of conscripts to obtain military personnel		
c) Business regulations		
i. Price controls: extent to which businesses are free to set their own prices		
ii. Administrative conditions and new businesses: administrative procedures are an important obstacle to starting a new business	19.	Minimum license fee for traders
iii. Time with govt. bureaucracy: senior management spends a substantial amount of time dealing with government bureaucracy	20.	Implementation rate of Industrial Entrepreneurs Memorandum (IEM denotes the intention to invest, but when there are bureaucratic or other delays the rate of implementation is lower)
iv. Starting a new business: starting a new business is generally easy	21.	Power shortage as a percentage of total demand (power shortage exists either due to low investment on the part of the government or due to low levels of private sector generation)
v. Irregular payments: irregular, payments connected with import and export permits, business licenses, exchange controls, tax assessments, police protection or loan applications are very rare.	22.	Cases pending investigation from previous year of cases registered under prevention of corruption and related acts as a share of total cases registered under the same acts
	23.	Persons arrested as a share of total cases being investigated under prevention of corruption and related acts

APPENDIX IV

Data and Results

APPENDIX TABLE IV.1

Area 1—Size of Government: Expenditures, Taxes and Enterprises, 2011

State	Inverse of Government Revenue Expenditure as a Share of Gross State Domestic Product (GSDP) (2009-10)	Inverse of Administrative GSDP as a ratio of Total GSDP (2009-10)	Inverse of Share of Government in Organised Employment (2010-11)	Inverse of State Level Taxes on Income as a Ratio of GDP (2009-10)	Inverse of Ratio of State Level Taxes on Property and Capital Transactions to State GDP (2009-10)	Inverse of State Level Taxes on Commodities and Services to GDP (2009-10)	Inverse of Stamp Duty Rate (2009-10)
Andhra Pradesh	7.68	0.30	1.54	1,269.2	34,619	36	0.20
Assam	6.49	0.13	2.07	593.1	34,972	21	0.12
Bihar	6.15	0.17	1.06	-	87,319	133	0.08
Chhattisgarh	7.96	0.30	1.11	14,299.9	41,003	61	0.13
Gujarat	11.08	0.32	2.39	2,310.4	40,803	46	0.13
Haryana	10.53	0.41	1.77	-	52,380	68	0.08
Himachal Pradesh	4.59	0.14	1.44	-	42,455	24	0.13
Jammu & Kashmir	3.47	0.07	1.06	-	135,138	34	-
Jharkhand	6.22	0.22	1.25	-	14,029	13	0.08
Karnataka	8.27	0.27	2.12	628.9	16,710	22	0.10
Kerala	8.16	0.24	1.85	19,241.1	22,209	34	0.12
Madhya Pradesh	7.35	0.19	1.17	1,190.9	25,684	40	0.13
Maharashtra	11.91	0.19	1.94	577.3	22,316	47	0.20
Orissa	7.66	0.22	1.17	1,447.0	43,641	52	0.07
Punjab	7.94	0.21	1.57	-	30,373	56	0.17
Rajasthan	7.44	0.22	1.31	-	29,678	39	0.10
Tamil Nadu	8.84	0.25	1.58	-	23,654	32	0.13
Uttar Pradesh	6.83	0.14	1.31	24,824.1	27,074	53	0.07
Uttaranchal	7.94	0.13	1.27	10,949.6	46,095	65	0.07
West Bengal	7.73	0.17	1.66	1,227.1	33,020	71	0.14

APPENDIX TABLE IV.2

Area 2—Legal Structure and Security of Property Rights,2011

State	Total Value of Property Recovered to the Total Value of Property Stolen (2010)	Inverse of Vacant Posts in the Judiciary to the Total Number of Sanctioned Judicial Posts (2010)	Inverse of Total Number of Cases under Economic Offences to the Total Number of Cases (2010)	Percentage of Cases where Trials were Completed by the Police (2010)	Percentage of Cases where Trials were Completed by the Courts (2010)	Inverse of Violent Crimes as a Ratio of Total Crimes (2010)
Andhra Pradesh	0.47	6.28	17.31	78.0	23.5	14.53
Assam	0.25	16.30	25.37	40.4	13.3	5.94
Bihar	0.14	4.05	30.73	50.5	9.1	5.30
Chhattisgarh	0.29	7.92	51.46	88.1	15.5	10.11
Gujarat	0.14	33.18	47.12	86.9	6.2	16.88
Haryana	0.53	3.30	22.65	80.6	18.8	8.91
Himachal Pradesh	0.32	25.20	30.21	80.5	8.2	9.82
Jammu & Kashmir	0.43	4.81	39.29	68.4	11.0	5.09
Jharkhand	0.13	3.11	25.77	55.5	28.9	4.56
Karnataka	0.41	7.15	22.96	69.5	21.6	8.64
Kerala	0.07	25.65	37.28	87.2	19.2	12.62
Madhya Pradesh	0.90	7.32	92.40	95.5	16.8	13.80
Maharashtra	0.10	7.45	18.89	64.2	6.2	9.15
Orissa	0.28	9.38	38.70	71.0	9.2	6.03
Punjab	0.61	3.53	9.53	65.9	18.2	9.10
Rajasthan	0.61	4.20	9.36	95.6	11.0	15.44
Tamil Nadu	0.50	19.71	49.54	67.8	32.0	15.06
Uttar Pradesh	0.40	8.04	12.63	88.3	22.5	6.40
Uttaranchal	0.38	1.95	12.05	89.0	16.2	5.82
West Bengal	0.23	6.06	28.90	62.2	4.0	6.41

APPENDIX TABLE IV.3

Area 3—Regulation of Labour and Business, 2011

State	Ratio of Average Wage of Unskilled Workers (Males) to Minimum Wages (2008-09)	Ratio of Average Wage of Unskilled Workers (Females) to Minimum Wages (2008-09)	Inverse of Man-days Lost in Strikes and Lockouts/Total Number of Industrial Workers (2009-10)	Inverse of Minimum License Fee for Traders (2009-10)	Implementation Rate of Industrial Entrepreneurs Memorandum (IEM) (2009)	Inverse of Power Shortage as a Percentage of Total Demand (2009)	Inverse of Pendency Rate of Cases Registered Under Corruption and Related Acts (2010)
Andhra Pradesh	1.09	-	2.76	0.04	0.031	0.92	2.15
Assam	1.14	1.05	4.38	0.10	0.055	0.91	1.04
Bihar	0.66	0.67	1.22	-	0.001	0.81	2.00
Chhattisgarh	1.14	1.18	4.28	0.00	0.003	0.85	1.58
Gujarat	1.41	1.02	9.17	0.20	0.088	0.97	1.98
Haryana	0.84	0.45	9.71	0.05	0.186	0.96	1.54
Himachal Pradesh	1.28	1.12	11.58	-	0.057	0.96	1.67
Jammu & Kashmir			14.75	-	0.136	0.65	1.33
Jharkhand	-	-	1.87	-	0.005	0.83	1.28
Karnataka	1.28	-	6.19	0.01	0.019	0.89	1.63
Kerala	1.44	0.56	1.39	-	0.090	0.92	1.47
Madhya Pradesh	1.06	2.18	1.75	0.00	0.034	0.98	2.19
Maharashtra	1.56	1.06	2.37	0.33	0.047	0.81	1.51
Orissa	1.20	0.85	1.18	-	0.002	0.99	1.70
Punjab	0.82	0.29	4.15	-	0.063	0.83	1.36
Rajasthan	0.84	0.00	0.32	0.01	0.106	0.96	1.47
Tamil Nadu	1.21	0.98	1.09	-	0.044	0.89	2.44
Uttar Pradesh	1.28	1.11	1.17	0.00	0.117	0.90	1.57
Uttaranchal	0.70	0.64	7.70	-	0.074	0.87	1.11
West Bengal	1.77	1.07	0.02	0.01	0.051	0.98	-

Friedrich-Naumann-Stiftung für die Freiheit

Friedrich-Naumann-Stiftung für die Freiheit (FNF) is the German foundation for liberal politics working for the promotion of ideas on liberty and strategies for freedom across the world. Its main instruments are civic education, political consultancy and political dialogue. FNF lends its expertise for endeavours to consolidate and strengthen freedom, democracy, market economy and the rule of law. As the only liberal organisation of its kind world-wide, the Foundation facilitates to lay the groundwork for a future in freedom that bears responsibility for the coming generations. Within South Asia, with its strong tradition of tolerance and love for freedom, with its growing middle classes which increasingly assert themselves, and with its liberalising economies, the Foundation works with numerous partner organisations to strengthen the structures of democracy, the rule of law, and the economic preconditions for social development and a life in dignity.

Friedrich-Naumann-Stiftung
India and Regional Office, South Asia
USO House, 6, Special Institutional Area
New Delhi 110067, India
Tel. +91-11-41688149
www.southasia.fnst.org

Cato Institute

The Cato Institute is a public policy research organisation dedicated to broadening the parameters of policy debate to allow consideration of more options that are consistent with the principles of individual liberty, limited government, free markets and peace. To that end, the Institute strives to achieve greater involvement of the intelligent, concerned lay public in questions of policy and the proper role of government through an extensive programme of publications and seminars on a wide range of domestic and international policy issues.

Cato Institute
1000 Massachusetts Ave., NW
Washington, DC 20001
Tel. 202 842-0200
www.cato.org

Indicus Analytics

Indicus Analytics is India's leading economics research and data analysis firm. Indicus examines many aspects of the Indian economy both at the national and sub-national level. It conducts monitoring and evaluation studies, indexation and ratings, as well as policy research. The endeavour of this research is to broaden the public policy debate to promote liberalism and the mechanisms of the market for the stimulation of growth in India. Our data products and research services are widely used by the top research and policy organisations, governments and corporates.

Indicus Analytics
2nd Floor, Nehru House
4 Bahadur Shah Zafar Marg
New Delhi 110002, India
Tel. +91-11-42512400
www.indicus.net

Academic Foundation

Academic Foundation (AF), based in New Delhi, is a leading publisher of academic/scholarly books in social sciences (area of specialisation: economics and allied). Guided by its motto *publishing to make a difference*, over the last few years of steady growth, AF has built a strong reputation for its publications on all fronts—editorial, production and marketing. Books published by Academic Foundation have global reach. Most notably, in addition to its own publications authored by some of the best known economists and scholars, Academic Foundation enjoys the privilege of having publishing tie-ups with numerous organisations and institutions of high repute. These include various departments/ministries of Government of India, a host of UN organisations, well known national and international NGOs, research bodies and so on.

Academic Foundation
4772-73/23 Bharat Ram Road,
(23 Ansari Road),
Darya Ganj,
New Delhi 110002, India
Tel. +91-11-23245001/02/03/04
www.academicfoundation.com